Otrarse

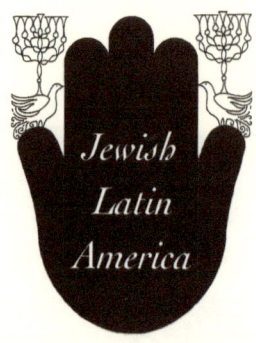

Jewish Latin America Series
ILAN STAVANS, Series Editor

The Jewish Latin America Series, relaunched in 2024, will introduce Jewish Latin American culture to a broad English-language readership. Through high-caliber translations as well as original English-language editions, it aims to open up a field of study by publishing classics as well as contemporary novels, memoirs, biographies, story collections, poetry, and anthologies. The series will map out the extraordinary creativity of the Jewish community in Latin America, from colonial times to the present, in a region far more diverse than is usually imagined.

Also available in the Jewish Latin America Series:

Otrarse

Ladino Poems

Juan Gelman

Edited and Translated by Ilan Stavans

Foreword by Ilya Kaminsky

UNIVERSITY of NEW MEXICO PRESS
Albuquerque

ISBN 978-0-8263-6679-5 (paper)
ISBN 978-0-8263-6680-1 (ePub)
ISBN 978-0-8263-6681-8 (webPDF)

Library of Congress Control Number: 2024944710

Founded in 1889, the University of New Mexico sits
    on the traditional homelands of the Pueblo of
    Sandia. The original peoples of New Mexico—
    Pueblo, Navajo, and Apache—since time
    immemorial have deep connections to the land
    and have made significant contributions to the
    broader community statewide. We honor the land
    itself and those who remain stewards of this land
    throughout the generations and also acknowledge
    our committed relationship to Indigenous peoples.
    We gratefully recognize our history.

Cover illustration: *Jánuca*, by José Gurvich. Courtesy
    of Martin Gurvich.
Designed by Isaac Morris
Composed in Arima, PF Marlet Display, and Tinos

To Peter Cole
—I. S.

palabra di una lingua pardida
aprovu intinderti

word of a lost language
I seek to understand you
—Clarisse Nicoïdski, *El color del tiempo* (2014)

Contents

Part Three. Com/positions
(from *Com/posiciones* [1986])

Part Four. Letter to My Mother (from *Carta a mi madre* [1989])

Part Five. *Lo judío* and Spanish-Language Literature (1992)

Part Six. Dibaxu (*Dibaxu* [1994])

Part Seven. Worth It (from *Vale la pena* [2001])

Notes
219

Index of First Lines
235

Foreword

ILYA KAMINSKY

Two Boys

"Poetry, can you recite some poetry?" They are two refugees, these young Jewish boys in the middle of the bustling neighborhood where mostly refugees live. It is the first half of the twentieth century. It is Argentina. "Some poetry, please," a younger six-year-old Juan repeats in Spanish, and his older brother, Boris, stuns him by responding with a full-throated recitation of verses in Russian by Aleksandr Pushkin.

The younger boy doesn't know Russian, but he is mesmerized by what he sees.

This is the first poetry reading in his life, and it happens in a language he does not know.

That is how the great poet of the Spanish language, Juan Gelman, first falls in love.

The Limits of Language

Fifty years have passed. We are now in Mexico City, where an old man, a famous exile, a poet and journalist, bends over a table filled with dictionaries.

He is teaching himself Ladino, a language of Sephardic Jews that is derived from Old Spanish and written in Hebrew letters.

There is something in this language he doesn't yet understand, a language that isn't his native, a language that resonates with his own exile, his own pain, something that calls to him—as he is turning the dictionary pages, opening another dictionary, closing it, beginning again.

What is it, that something?

He is writing *Dibaxu*—a book of poems that opens the windows of the present to the era of the Spanish Inquisition, to his people centuries ago, surviving in Sephardic diaspora as they flee. *Dibaxu*, a book composed after many years of translating poets of medieval Spain, translating also psalms, hymns—so many years of translating by a man who says, more than once, that he doesn't believe in translation.

"The tongue expands a language in order to better converse with itself," Juan Gelman announced in his well-known Cervantes speech. "These inventions beat in the bowels of the tongue, and generate babbles and breezes of infancy, like some memory of words that comes from beyond."

Perhaps. But what is this "expansion of language"? What does it mean for a man who fell in love with poetry by listening to it in a language he did not know? What does it mean for a man who spent many years translating others while declaring a fraught relationship to translation? What is translation, in Juan Gelman's case? Is it bringing other poets into a new language? Or is it bringing the new language into other poets? And what is translation for *any* practicing writer? Is this translation a way of revising one's self?

"These new words, are they not a victory against the limits of language? Does the air not continue to speak to us?" he continues in his Cervantes speech. "There are millions of nameless places, and poetry works to name what is still unnamed."

Perhaps. Rereading Gelman's own rereadings of other poets in light of his desire to test the limits of language, I can't help but be reminded of an image from Kabbalah where before beginning a prayer the man makes himself a robe out of written verses of prayers, and, wearing that robe, he makes the prayer as he chants it.

The Dirty War

Yes, we began with the image of a six-year-old boy falling in love with poetry. Born of Jewish Ukrainian refugees in Buenos Aires, he grows up amid many languages in a neighborhood where refugees struggle to make a life. Yes, for him the struggle for a life and the fascination with words, with the limits of language itself, become a lifelong duet.

But what is the context of all this? What happens between this moment of the six-year-old Juan Gelman first listening, stunned, as his brother Boris recites poetry in a language Juan does not understand, and Juan Gelman, the grand old poet, learning a new (ancient) language so he could write "new words" in it?

During these years we find him in the roles of an activist, a revolutionary, and a journalist, and he serves time in jail for his political work. During these years he also pens dozens of books. But the defining event of this time is the

Dirty War—as a military dictatorship forms death squads to hunt down and murder thousands of political dissidents in his country, our poet witnesses his own son and daughter-in-law being "disappeared" by the state.

Yes, his son Marcelo, a twenty-year-old journalist, and his nineteen-year-old daughter-in-law Maria Claudia are "disappeared." They are among an estimated thirty thousand people who vanished into torture chambers or were dropped to their deaths from airplanes. Maria Claudia was seven months pregnant at the time. During this time, Gelman had spent many years of exile trying to locate this lost child.

A "Difficult" Poet

These are the years of long exile, yes. The years when, as he told one journalist, only in the poetry of others he could find a respite: "Out of the country," he confided in a 2009 conversation with the *Café Review*, "I translated poets of past centuries. It was a form of consolation."

And his writing? "I write poetry because I have no other remedy," he said to the *Millions*.

So, what it is, this remedy, this poetry? Gelman isn't as popular as some of his contemporaries. Critics call him a "complex" poet, a "difficult" poet—but this "difficulty" of style happens during a moment of extreme historical, social, and political difficulty. It is also echoed by the centuries of difficulty that this poet's people had to survive during exiles and pogroms. So it is not a stretch to suggest that the complexity of this style mirrors the complexity of historical process as well as the complexity of what everyone in the poet's country had to go through during the period of "disappearances." This is not to say that every complex author lives in a time of civic strife, but if the author's family is abducted and killed, if this author himself happens to be a child of refugees from pogroms, might there be a whole other level of meaning to his need to speak to the dead, to speak in tongues, to reach for "new words," reach for a language across the boundaries of time and space, and perhaps call this—maybe even against his own better judgement—a translation?

Perhaps. In the spirit of meanings that are behind meanings, I want to quote a poem of Gelman's that is not in this book but is translated by Ilan Stavans and published in his *Selected Translations*. For here is Gelman's own definition of poetry, and it presents his case with more clarity and passion than anyone else's introduction:

Poetry is a way of living.

Look at the people at your side.

Do they eat? Suffer? Sing? Cry?

Help them fight for their hands, their eyes, their mouth, for the kiss to kiss and the kiss to give away, for their table, their bread, their letter *a* and their letter *h*, for their past—were they not children?—for their present, for the piece of peace, of history and happiness, that belongs to them, for the piece of love, big, small, sad, joy, that belongs to them and is taken away in the name of what, of what?

Your life will then be an innumerable river to be called pedro, juan, ana, maria, bird, lung, the air, my shirt, violin, sunset, stone, that handkerchief, old waltz, wooden horse.

Poetry is this.

Afterward, write it.

Giving a Name

But what is the lesson here? What do we learn from all this talking to the dead across time and space? What does this poet bring to the table? What is his contribution? Knowing the time when this poet wrote his work, the circumstances during which it happened, I find myself quite moved when I read, in the passage quoted above: "Your life will then be an innumerable river to be called pedro, juan, ana, maria, bird, lung, the air, my shirt, violin, sunset, stone, that handkerchief, old waltz, wooden horse."

As I reread this, I find myself wanting to go back to Gelman's very late poems. Professor Stavans gives us a taste in the final two pages of this book. These are poems written by a man who already declared to us that "poetry is a way of living." They are written after all the labors of translations, after all the hard work of reimagining the self, all the work of survival (survival in exile, a man's survival in the face of the death of his child and the disappearance of his grandchild) through language. It is as if they meet us on the other side, these two poems. It is as if a six-year-old boy, now in the body of an old man, looks back and sees the measures by which we are all seen:

Measures

Grandfather looks at me from
the usual photo, he looks at me
from the depths of Russia and other misfortunes.
From the ghetto he looks at me. They
say he wrote a letter to God to
flood the houses with wheat,
wine and matzah on Passover,
and tied the letter to a bird's foot
which flew from country to country looking for heaven.
He looks at me with the slow sleepy ears
of someone who mourned terror. Grandfather
never picked me up in his arms. I never
had him, he never
had me. Never
is our agreed word. He wanted
truth to wander through the street
and covered it with a mask
so as to be wanted.
Grandfather must have asked God not
to commit anything into writing or erase it because
things could get worse. The photo
is sick, raising
a cloud of smoke made of arms unable to greet each other,
handcuffing its ancestry,
haunting me like a dog.

Haunting, indeed. This is a poem written in the years when Gelman is himself a grandfather, the years when (as he confessed to one journalist) a "happy" ending took place—he was reunited with his granddaughter, the child of his "disappeared" son, the girl who was stolen from him for many years. Who is this "grandfather" spoken about in this poem? Is it Gelman himself, or is it also his granddaughter's voice—the future's voice—being channeled?

Grandfather
never picked me up in his arms. I never
had him, he never
had me. Never
is our agreed word. He wanted
truth to wander through the street
and covered it with a mask
so as to be wanted.
Grandfather must have asked God not
to commit anything into writing or erase it because
things could get worse.

Who is speaking here? I come back to Gelman's Cervantes speech: "the poet's tongue expands a language in order to converse with itself."

"These new words, are they not a victory against the limits of language?" Gelman asks. Through his life, despite countless changes around him, he keeps searching for the new language. "There are millions of nameless places, and poetry works to name what is still unnamed." Names. No wonder this is the last poem in this book.

Names

My father's name was José.
Why José?
Why was he called José? I must
stop him with the question:
Why were you called José? There goes
my looking at you as if you never wanted
to share a soul with me. The word
is a loss of words
in a woman's face.
I have seen it in parades of error.
And sometimes I sit down
to wait for his absence.
When the day is nothing more
than such illness,

the sun refuses to sun. The unfinished
announcement of something unknown
descends with the afternoon as I see
the bed where you died
and your silence that won't die.
Why José?
Why were you called José?

On some days even "the sun refuses to sun," yes. But the poet's search continues. Because the "silence won't die," because the "soul" must be "shared" via language. The new words must be found to do this, because the poem ends with a question, with its ongoing search.

Ilan Stavans's Gelman

Great poets deserve many translators. And, in fact, there are many Gelmans: the poet has been translated in numerous languages, and several terrific English translations exist. But I have been carrying Ilan Stavans's great recreation of Gelman's Ladino poems with me for a while now. Stavans's introductory essay alone is a truly important work, comparable in breadth and scope to John Felstiner's monumental approach to Paul Celan. First of all, Stavans's perspective is *interesting*—something one doesn't always say about such texts. Stavans's passion is contagious, and Gelman's life story and literary journey are truly gripping. It is a rabbit hole one happily falls into, relishing every moment.

For, dear reader, in the pages that follow, we are in presence of something marvelous: one of our best critical minds here introduces one of the twentieth century's most fascinating poets, whose own journey was a conversation with poetics across the boundaries of time and space.

Yes, Gelman was a revolutionary poet and a man of letters whose work was dedicated to those who disappeared under Argentina's junta. Yes, his voice is incredibly relevant to our own moment of crisis. But what is also crucial—and beautifully discussed here by Stavans, who is our time's great ambassador for poetry—is the spiritual aspect of Gelman's work, which is inseparable from, and in fact propulsive of, the poet's innovative perspective and his awareness of truth seeking.

A student of the ages-old Ladino mystic tradition ("you are / my only world / I know not your name," he wrote as he studied the new language), a midrashic poet intent on stating his interest in "opening the doors of time," Gelman wanted to reveal to us new meanings of praise and lament. And that he did.

But this book does more: here, Ilan Stavans gently but with much nuance transforms our North American perspective on the Jewish presence in Spanish-language literature. If you have opened this volume in a bookstore, I suggest you read Stavans's stunning introduction, followed by Gelman's essay, *"Lo judío* and Spanish-Language Literature,"* then reread the two final and very moving lyrics, "Measures" and "Names," and I assure you that, like myself, you won't be able to let go of *Otrarse*. Ilan Stavans's Gelman is extraordinary.

Introduction

Becoming *Sefardí*

ILAN STAVANS

La verdad sufre, pero nunca muere.

Truth suffers but never dies.
—Santa Teresa de Jesús

I

In a region known for its politically engaged poets, Juan Gelman was one of the most incisive Latin American poets of the twentieth century as well as one of the most innovative. In more than twenty poetry collections published between 1956 and his death in 2014, he addressed, without trepidation, the most pressing topic of his native Argentina and of the continent: the excesses of the region's dictatorial regimes, the state violence they orchestrated, and the erasure of dissidence and the dismantling of collective memory. For this, Gelman was arrested during the period known as Guerra Sucia (the Dirty War), as was his family. He was forced into exile, where he lived for almost the rest of his life.

Gelman returned to Argentina when democracy was reinstated, but only briefly. Exile by then had become a much more comfortable condition for him. Still, his quest for truth, justice, and democracy didn't stop. He was a major player in the Juicio de las Juntas (Trial of the Juntas), the process whereby the military figures responsible for the coup d'état that had pushed Argentina to the abyss in 1974 were brought to the martial courts. By the time Gelman reached old age, aside from his standing as a literary giant, receiving some of the most important prizes for Spanish-language literature (including the Premio Reina Sofía and Premio Cervantes), he had become a symbol of hope and change in Latin America.

Commentators often equate him with Pablo Neruda in his role as the people's poet, a witness of the ups and downs of the epoch in which he lived. The comparison is appropriate, although Gelman's works never sold millions of copies, like Neruda's *Twenty Love Poems and a Song of Despair* (1924) or *Canto General* (1950), in part because they are at times stylistically complex. Another suitable comparison is with early twentieth-century Peruvian exiled poet César Vallejo, author of *Spain, Take This Chalice from Me* (1937), whose oeuvre is infused with recurrent Catholic motifs. For instance, Vallejo wrote poems about the Spanish Civil War that have the feeling of being hymns. Faith and the afterlife were Vallejo's concerns, even when he criticized the Catholic Church for its oppressive role during the Spanish conquest of the Americas. Gelman, too, was in direct dialogue with religion, in his case Judaism, although he wasn't devout. As he announced time and again, he didn't believe in God. Why should he when, as he put it, God didn't seem to care one bit for the suffering of humans? Still, he used Jewish tradition and was attached to biblical and medieval Hebrew sources, and to the poetry of converso mystics like Santa Teresa de Ávila and San Juan de la Cruz, who lived under the shadow of the Holy Inquisition, to refashion a message of courage and internal exploration amid oppression.

Gelman understood poetry as a mechanism whereby truth is reached through an exercise of peeling away layers upon layers of falsehood. That process of finding truth might be connected to the relationship between lovers, or between parents and children, or between political leaders and their constituents in a democratic system established on the principles of social justice, or even between an individual and the cosmos. Truth, he knew, might be painful to accept. He didn't see poetry as therapy but as revelation: what needs to be known makes us free.

Indeed, Gelman was a midrashic poet. The exegetical method known as midrash (from the Hebrew verb *darash*, דָּרַשׁ, meaning to seek, to enquire) is designed to comprehend the dimensions of an emotion, or to dissect an ancient text dealing with an enduring topic in a way that makes both the text and the topic significant to present readers. It is poetry as a hermeneutical endeavor: to be useful, the poet—to use another metaphor—must dig deep into history, personal and collective, or into the conundrums of the present, for these are realms where others seldom go.

It isn't surprising, therefore, that Gelman had a lifelong interest in translation, for translation is about digging deep and peeling away, and about revealing meaning. To translate is much more than simply to move a text from one linguistic ecosystem to another; it is to uncover the truths in that text, to make it, in midrashic terms, palatable to a new audience. Ironically, just as Gelman wasn't a conventional poet, he was anything but a traditional translator. He was rather skeptical of translation. In the exergue to his volume *Com/positions* (1986), he argued that "to translate is inhuman" and that, since "no language or face lets itself be translated," it is imperative that we accept that "untouched beauty must be left alone."

II

Gelman's poetic approach sparked into maturity when a couple of pivotal events in his life made him change course. The first was in 1975, when the need came to go into exile from Argentina, his country, because of his left-leaning political activities. A coup d'état had deposed president Isabel Perón, known as Isabelita, Juan Domingo Perón's third wife. The military junta behind the coup quickly joined a CIA-orchestrated campaign known as Operación Cóndor to eradicate, by any means possible, what it deemed "subversive" forces. In subsequent years, around thirty thousand people would become desaparecidos. Thousands of others would go into exile. A considerable percentage of the desaparecidos were Jewish. In his long exile, Gelman lived in numerous countries, including Italy, Spain, Mexico, and the United States.

The second event that sparked Gelman's poetry happened the following year, in 1976. On August 24, Gelman's son Marcelo, twenty years old, along with his daughter-in-law María Claudia García Irureta Goyena, nineteen, were kidnapped in Buenos Aires by the military regime, allegedly for their left-wing activities. They were taken to the concentration camp Automotores Orletti, in the city's Floresta neighborhood, which the junta called El Jardín, the garden. Marcelo died with a gunshot to the back of his head. His body was placed in a barrel with sand and cement and thrown into the San Fernando River. His remains were not found until 1990. At the time of the kidnapping, María Claudia was six months pregnant. After a stay at Orletti, she was moved to Uruguay, whose right-wing government worked in tandem with Argentina's dictatorship. She was held at the clandestine Centro de Detención del Servicio de Información de Defensa. Upon the birth of her baby, she was moved to the Hospital Militar. Her remains are still missing.

In Buenos Aires, Juan Gelman had been a dissident journalist and the editor of various left-leaning newspapers. He also had been a member of the Montoneros, a Peronist guerrilla organization. Up until then, his Jewishness wasn't significant to him. Maybe it had fostered his passion for reading, but he didn't see Jewish literature—liturgy, poetry, fiction—as significant to him. What he was certain about was that as a poet his role was to denounce moral bankruptcy.

However, in the solitude of exile Gelman suddenly sensed a strong affinity with the intellectual and religious effervescence in Spain in the sixteenth century. He was prone to Santa Teresa de Ávila (1515–1582), a nun of the Carmelite order from the northwestern region of Castile and León who lived during the Counter-Reformation and who, as a prominent mystic and religious reformer, pushed for monastic renewal. Santa Teresa was the descendant of conversos who had been forced by the Holy Office of the Inquisition to embrace Catholicism. Aside from mesmerizing poems, she wrote an autobiographical manual called *The Dwellings; or, The Interior Castle* (1577), in which she proposed a spiritual journey of reaching the divine by going through four stages of spiritual ascent: the first is a stage of prayer and meditation; the second is a stage of quiet and contemplation; the third involves absorption of God (or better, absorption *in* God); and the fourth stage is about ecstatic consciousness.

Intriguingly, Santa Teresa's Christian mysticism, her methodology for reaching the chambers of divine glory, is not unlike the one traced by Moisés ben Jacob Cordovero (1522–1570), a leader of a mystical school in Safed, then in Ottoman Syria. Cordovero, one of the most important Jewish mystics, also offered a series of steps for reaching elevated levels of spiritual consciousness. In Cordovero's view, all things emanate from a perfect God, who represents the complete *ohr*, light (אור). As that light evolves, it gives place to seven imperfect lights. The process of reaching God is thus a journey of perfection, an ascendance to the original light.

The connection between Jewish and Christian mystics fascinated Gelman. He wasn't interested in spiritual purification but in emotional distillation. Emulating the writing of Santa Teresa and her pupil San Juan de la Cruz, he wrote poems about love between two individuals as an exalted encounter. Poetry could analyze that encounter by peeling away misconceptions. Along the way, what interested Gelman wasn't Santa Teresa's religious odyssey but her intricacies of being a conversa, that is, belonging to a people who hid their original religious identity. Santa Teresa, in Gelman's view, was a secret Jew in a Carmelite custom.

Gelman invented a term, *otrarse*, by which he meant "to become someone else." He realized that he had an affinity for pariahs: in this case, Jews in private, Christians in public. His tributes to the medieval mystics give the impression of being composed by a dybbuk, a dislocated, deceitful soul in someone else's body. They offer the reader a chance to see life through the veil of impostorship. He was compelled by the Carmelite nun's idea that as a believer she was exiled from God's love.

Gelman discovered that followers of certain trends in Jewish mysticism believed that God, called in Hebrew Ein Sof, meaning the infinite, was exiled from the universe he had created. This attraction encouraged Gelman to write poetry in a ventriloquist way, as if he himself were Santa Teresa. The result was a series of intricate poems based on *The Dwellings*. He followed them with rewritings of another Catholic mystic and one of Santa Teresa's pupils, San Juan de la Cruz (1542–1591). The outcome was a collection called *Quotes and Commentaries* (1979), in which Gelman's midrashic imagination linked the experience of Gelman as a political poet of the twentieth century with artistic motifs in fashion half a millennium earlier.

In 2007, as part of Gelman's acceptance speech upon receiving the Premio Cervantes, the most important literary award in the Spanish-language world, he stated that reading Santa Teresa and San Juan allowed him to experience emotions he didn't know he could verbalize, namely "la presencia ausente de lo amado, Dios para ellos, el país del que fui expulsado para mí," the absent presence of what we love, God for them, the country Gelman was expelled from for him. He said that exile, to paraphrase Santa Teresa, "no es sino morir muchas veces," is nothing but a way of dying repeatedly.

III

American poet Edward Hirsch, author of *Gabriel: A Poem* (2014), once said that Gelman "is an unwavering poet of conscience—his work is dedicated to the disappeared—but his lamentations keep giving way to praise of the renewable world." The key word here is *lamentation*. Gelman found the laments of the biblical prophets extraordinarily resonant. He also read more conversos, such as Fray Luis de León (1527–1591), who wrote a study of the Song of Songs.

This, in turn, made Gelman delve into the piyyutim, the liturgical poems produced by medieval Hebrew poets from al-Andalus, the southern region of the Iberian Peninsula. In his eyes, the imagery of Samuel Hanagid (993–1056), Solomon ibn Gabirol (ca. 1022–ca. 1070), and Yehuda Halevi (1075–1141) was mesmerizing—a mirror of his own passions. And he studied the poetic architecture of Kabbalah through the oeuvre of major theoreticians Isaac Luria and Abraham Abulafia. Overall, Gelman felt countless parallels between his own departure from Argentina in 1975 and the expulsion of the Jews from Spain in 1492. In both cases, an explosive history had pushed the poets of their respective epochs to see exile through a spiritual lens.

At the most intimate level, all this was about Gelman's Jewishness, an aspect of his persona he kept for himself. Born in 1930, Gelman was the child of Russian-speaking Ukrainian immigrants to Buenos Aires. His father, José (in Hebrew, Yosef) Gelman, married with two children, was a communist labor activist in the Russian revolution of 1905. His political activities forced him to leave for Argentina, leaving his wife and children behind. After the triumph of the Bolsheviks in 1917, he returned to Europe but wasn't allowed to enter the Soviet Union. From Berlin, he arranged for his family's exit from Moscow, but the boat they sailed in capsized, and his wife and one of the children died. Boris, the surviving son, waited for his father in Russia, to where José Gelman returned 1922, when he met Gelman's mother, Paulina Burichson. They married and had a daughter, Teodora. Together with Boris, the four moved to Argentina in 1928, a couple of years before Juan's birth.

All this back-and-forth movement explains why Gelman always claimed: "I'm the only Argentine in my family." Dissidence was in his blood. In Buenos Aires, the Gelmans settled in Villa Crespo, an ethnic enclave where not only Jews but Arabs from the Ottoman Empire coexisted. The milieu made him feel "como un otro," like an outsider, different from the Argentine mainstream. As a child, he was exposed to Russian, his mother tongue, in which his older brother Boris read him Pushkin's poetry and the novels of Tolstoy and Dostoevsky. In the neighborhood, he heard Yiddish, Ukrainian, and Ladino, the latter also known as *judeo-espaniol*, *judesmo*, or *sefardí*, a language derived from Old Spanish originally spoken in Spain and, after the expulsion in 1492, throughout the Ottoman Empire (the Balkans, Turkey, Greece, and North Africa), France, Italy, the Netherlands, Morocco, England, and communities throughout the Americas, aside, of course, from Israel, where the largest concentration of speakers is to be found. Plus, Gelman spoke Spanish. Then, as a young man, he learned English, Italian, French, and other tongues. That is what Gelman's exile would later on be about: translingualism.

It was the death of his son Marcelo that first pushed Gelman to use poetry as a mechanism to communicate with the dead. He did it in the form of an *Open Letter* (1980), arguably among the most syntactically intricate work he ever produced. As a literary genre, the letter allowed Gelman to be both private and public in his poetic inquiry. Six years later, he returned to the epistolary form when his mother died. Like *Todesfuge* (1948), Paul Celan's classic poem about the horrors of Auschwitz, Gelman's unqualified masterpiece, *Letter to My Mother*, is about the visceral encounter, in his imagination, with the corpse of mother, with whom he nurtures a zigzagging relationship that goes from love to anxiety and from guilt to silence. Intriguingly, Jewishness is almost totally absent from the work, at least openly. The same absence happens in a couple of other genealogical poems he wrote later in his career, one about a photograph of his father hanging in his childhood home, the other about family names.

The method of using poetry to unearth difficult fragments of truth is crystal clear in *Letter to My Mother*. This extended poem feels at once therapeutic in its drive to understand the twists and turns of a mother/son relationship and spiritual not in its search for the divine but in its intent to free the narrator from layers of emotional guilt accumulated over a lifetime. The language is raw, unapologetic. The waves of anxiety that serve as building blocks in the narrative accumulate in merciless fashion. At various points, Gelman, in what might be one of the best examples of "otrarse," becomes his own mother, just as his mother becomes him. As the poem reaches its climax, the reader no longer distinguishes these two individuals as separate entities. Ventriloquism here isn't about entering someone else's persona; it is about letting go of one's own in order to understand things in the most elemental way.

IV

Gelman was intrigued by the buried Jewish reservoir at the heart of Hispanic culture, which, because of anti-Semitism, often goes unacknowledged. It goes without saying that he wasn't Sephardic but Ashkenazi, tracing his descent to eastern Europe. (In Spanish, the word *sefardí* might be used as a noun to describe the Ladino language or as a demonym that refers to a person from Sepharad, סְפָרַד, the Hebrew word used in the Bible for Spain.) Gelman had heard Ladino as a child in Villa Crespo but considered himself an outsider toward it. Still, he felt its magnetism. He didn't know Hebrew but loved folktales about the Hebrew letters. In an essay titled "The Last Letter," he meditated on Moisés de León (1240–1305), the author of the *Book of Zohar* (thirteenth century), the fundamental Kabbalistic treatise. To validate his writings, which de León felt wouldn't be taken seriously by the rabbinical community, he pretended that his book was a palimpsest composed by the second-century scholar Rabbi Yohanan ben Zakkai (circa the year 100), a Talmudic sage from the late Second Temple period.

Gelman fixated on a single chapter of the *Zohar*, "The Secret of the Letters," in which readers are told that before the universe was created, the twenty-two letters of the Hebrew alphabet paraded before the divine presence to make a case about the order they should follow. After much debate, God decided that Aleph would be the first in the alphabet and Bet would open the first chapter of Genesis. Equally tantalizing for Gelman was the fact that, according to the *Zohar*, there is actually a twenty-third Hebrew letter, but that letter will only make itself apparent after Tikkun Olam, the mending of the world, when messianic times will be upon us.

After *Quotes and Commentaries* came *Com/positions*. In it, Gelman literally rewrote a number of medieval Hebrew poems in his own style. This sequence is a veritable feast of hermeneutical prowess. To achieve his goal, he paired down the Spanish language to a bare minimum. Indeed, I estimate the total size of Gelman's lexicon in this volume to be no more than two hundred different words. No capital letters are used. Line breaks are idiosyncratic. Periods are nonexistent. And the use of slashes creates blocks of meaning.

Tangentially, some of Gelman's inspiration comes from deconstructionism, the French school of literary criticism popular in the 1980s that was led by Jacques Derrida and Julia Kristeva, two scholars of Sephardic ancestry. Gelman thought their work was obtuse. But he was interested in intertextuality. That is what drew him to medieval figures like Dunash ben Labrat (ca. 920–ca. 990), a medieval Jewish commentator, poet, and grammarian, and his rival Menahem ibn Saruk (ca. 920–ca. 970), a Judeo-Spanish philologist. Gelman was mesmerized by their technique of astutely inserting a single biblical line, maybe even an entire verse, into a new poem. The quotation might be literal, lightly altered, or elliptical, creating a whole gamut of effects from the allusive to the comical.

Gelman experimented with the technique, recomposing poems by Hanagid, ibn Gabirol, Halevi, Luria, and others. The result was exhilarating. Gelman quickly found out that originality is a game of hide-and-seek. He applied the same ventriloquist approach to rewritings of psalms attributed to King David, and to poetic sections in the Bible that belong to the books of prophets such as Amos, Isaiah, and Ezekiel. Shrewdly, in his midrashic quest Gelman devised a method to incorporate translation by not engaging directly with it. He returned to the concept of "otrarse," to become another. By becoming King David, Halevi, and Santa Teresa—by using their voice as his own—he was able to peel at the layers that often obscure truth.

I agree with Uruguayan journalist Eduardo Galeano, author of *Open Veins of Latin America* (1971), that no one in Spanish sounds like Gelman. And I think Julio Cortázar, the legendary counterculture Argentine novelist responsible for *Hopscotch* (1967), is right when he argued that Gelman creates a "contralengua," a counterlanguage. "It is not easy to enter—from line one—into a discourse that travels against the current," Cortázar posits, "even to the point where it tramples without shame over the most stringent rules of our mental well-being." That counterlanguage is the prime example of what Gelman means by *otrarse*:

He turns nouns like *dictadura* (dictatorship) into verbs like *dictadurar* (dictatorshipping). He concocts neologisms (*miedara, desquerer, hijando, perradura*) and compound words (*musicanta, morirvivirme, cuerpoalma*). Not to mention his consistent use of the Argentine second-personal singular *vos* (*podés, herís, decís*). Gelman rejects capitalization and plays with repetition in labyrinthine ways. More dramatically, his idiosyncratic punctuation resembles that of Emily Dickinson: periods are out, commas barely show up, and the forward slash becomes inventive to fracture language and make room for silence. And in general, he reinvents grammar. The effect is stunnihg.

There is also what I call Gelman's Pessoan self. Fernando Pessoa, the Portuguese author of *The Book of Disquiet* (published posthumously in 1982), spent his career creating heteronyms and fictional authors (Ricardo Reis, Alberto Caeiro, Álvaro de Campos, Bernardo Soares, Alexander Search, et al.), and publishing literary works under these names. Gelman did something similar. He invented at least one medieval poet, Eliezer ben Jonon. He inserted several poems he credited to ben Jonon in *Com/positions*, passing them as originals of an impostor, a nonexistent author. This gave Gelman even more freedom to play with his own Jewishness.

V

I move now from talking about Gelman's work to the content of the present volume and about my own translations and impostorships. I vehemently disagree with Gelman's characterization of translation as an impossible task; otherwise, this anthology wouldn't exist, even though Gelman's ornamented simplicity resists traveling across languages. Aware of—maybe obsessed with— Paul Valéry's dictum that "fidelity in meaning alone in translation is a form of betrayal," my renditions are truthful to his originals while making room for the Hebrew, Spanish, Ladino, and even English echoes buried in them: from the King James Version in 1611 to Santa Teresa's *The Dwellings* in 1588 to Emma Lazarus's renditions of Moses ibn Ezra via the German poet Heinrich Heine in the late nineteenth century to T. Carmi's *The Penguin Book of Hebrew Verse* in 1981 to Robert Alter's *The Hebrew Bible* in 2019.

My interest is simultaneously poetic and archaeological: I seek to create objects of beauty while also retracing the foundations (biblical, liturgical, Talmudic, theological, and so on) on which Gelman's poems are built. The material is organized chronologically. In the notes located in the back matter, I map Gelman's readings, look at the way he built his poems, and trace the resonance of individual lines as they manifest themselves at different moments in time. All this make my versions not translations but re-creations.

In a keynote address delivered Buenos Aires in June 1992 titled "*Lo judío* in Spanish-Language Literature," part of a conference of Jewish writers from Latin America, Gelman stated that, effectively, he believed there is a hidden Jewish current in Hispanic civilization, even though that current is seldom recognized. Indeed, the only other writer who mapped Jewishness in Spanish is Jorge Luis Borges, another Argentine and Gelman's elder by about three decades. His stories "The Aleph," "The Secret Miracle," "Emma Zunz," and "Deutsches Requiem" analyze various aspects of *lo judío*, as he did in essays and poems about golems, Baruch Spinoza, Franz Kafka, Zionism, and other themes. Yet Borges wasn't Jewish, although he wished that he were. Gelman, in contrast, delved unapologetically into his own genealogy in order to *judaizar*, to Judaize the Spanish language. In the keynote, he actually suggested that the cadre of medieval poets he recycled had used their own bodies to be free, a stunning image when one recalls that the Inquisition tortured crypto-Jews for not being like everyone else.

The climactic moment in Gelman's drive toward Jewish self-discovery started a few years before the conference of Jewish writers from Latin America, in 1989, when he lived in Paris. He stumbled upon a book by an obscure French author by the name of Clarisse Nicoïdski. She had written novels in French but her poetic oeuvre was in Ladino, her mother tongue. Like Gelman, Nicoïdski's verses are visceral, reconfiguring syntactical patterns. She was obsessed with exile, with translingualism, and with a feeling of inescapable solitude. Gelman fell in love with her work.

What is more, he was overwhelmed by the unstoppable need to learn Ladino. Doing so would allow him to become a full-fledged citizen of Sephardic civilization. At first, he hesitated, given his role as outsider. Would his urge lead him to become an imposter? He didn't want to be seen as appropriating another Jewish tradition. The Shoah had already done enormous damage to that Jewish cultural lineage. Yet he couldn't stop. Years of exile had convinced him that outsiders, at their core, are dutiful, invaluable witnesses.

"The extreme solitude of exile had pushed me to search for roots in the language," Gelman stated, "the deepest and most exiled of the language." In time, Gelman composed a sequence of twenty-nine short poems called *Dibaxu*, a Ladino word meaning "under." Reading Nicoïdski had awakened in him "una sorda necesidad," a deaf urge eager to wake up. "What urge? Why was it asleep? Why deaf?" He responded by saying that Ladino syntax gave him back "a lost candor: its diminutives, a tenderness toward others that is alive and full of comfort"—all this made him feel at home.

In fact, while learning Ladino Gelman discovered that everything he had done in connection with Jewish themes already had the DNA of that language. He was, in essence, an honorary *sefardí*. Once he finished *Dibaxu*, he did something that surprised him even more: he translated his Ladino poems into Spanish, reversing his moratorium on self-translation, suddenly allowed himself to artfully travel back and forth between linguistic universes. His Spanish versions weren't translations per se; they were actually second originals. Gelman stated that he accompanied every Ladino text with present-day Spanish "not out of distrust for the reader's intelligence, but for them to be read aloud in Spanish and listened to in Ladino, in the hope that maybe in between these two sounds a glimpse of the trembling past since El Cid comes back to us."

The trembling past—a gorgeous image. Gelman's road to Tikkun Olam came in 1988. Democracy in Argentina was back. Initiatives to put the military generals responsible for the atrocities during the Dirty War in prison were on their way. With his arrest warrant nullified, Gelman returned from his wandering life abroad to Argentina that summer for the first time in thirteen years. But he realized that a life outside his home was more suitable to him, and he settled in Mexico. A year later, Gelman was pardoned by Argentina's President Carlos Menem, but he preferred to maintain his home in Mexico. When he died in 2014 at the age of eighty-three, he was recognized as one of the most important Latin American poets of the twentieth century. Argentina's president at that time, Cristina Fernández de Kirchner, declared three days of mourning.

By then, his *contralengua* had been translated into numerous languages, though not, to my knowledge, into Yiddish, Hebrew, or Ladino. But his midrashic journey continues unexplored, as a result, perhaps, of the ongoing disinterest, in the Spanish-speaking world, for things Jewish. Proof of that is that *Com/position* has been translated into English, in full or in part, at least three times. None of those efforts mention Gelman's Jewishness. It is like enjoying Shakespeare without acknowledging that he was English.

A couple of decades into his exile, on April 12, 1995, Gelman published an open letter addressed to his grandchild, whose mother had died and who had been given for adoption by the military. Democracy had come back to Argentina in 1983. Almost immediately, elected president Raúl Alfonsín created the National Commission on the Disappearance of Persons, charged with investigated human rights violations committed during the Dirty War. The commission created a report, *Nunca más* (Never Again), which included individual cases on nine thousand disappeared persons and which served as the blueprint of the Trial of the Juntas, a war-crimes trial conducted by a civilian court—the first such trial since the Nuremberg trials after the Second World War.

Gelman, still convulsed by the dismantling of morality in the country, remained abroad. He was behind the drive to sort out the fate of the desaparecidos, which was a primary obligation of the new period. His story became a referendum on the nation's need to reconcile with its atrocious past. In time, Gelman identified his son's remains. His open letter allowed him to reconnect with his granddaughter Macarena, who had been raised by a right-wing Uruguayan family. Macarena eventually changed her last name to Gelman.

VI

Gelman's ventriloquism belongs to a larger aesthetic attitude in modern Latin America. Occasionally referred to as "cannibalism," this attitude has been practiced by prominent poets, such as Brazil's famous twentieth-century sibling poets Haroldo and Augusto de Campos, who, at different moments in their careers, re-created foreign poems by "devouring" their meaning, chewing it up, and spitting it out in a totally different form. The de Campos brothers traced their approach to Oswaldo de Andrade, a late nineteenth-century cultural critic, poet, and novelist from São Paolo, who, in his "Cannibalist Manifesto" (1928), argued that Brazil, with its history of colonial dependency, had no other option but to outright steal (*roubar*) and swallow (*engolir*) from Europe to find its own unique artistic voice. In *Verso, reverso, controverso* (1978), a collection of Augusto de Campos's translations of medieval poets and others, he states: "I'm only interested in what is not mine . . . the untranslated and the untranslatable."

Other Latin American poets have been equally unconventional in their translations. Mexican Nobel Prize winner Octavio Paz translated E. E. Cummings in ways that resemble more his own style than that of the American poet. José Emilio Pacheco, also Mexican, titled his translations of Dante, Omar Khayyám, Lewis Carroll, Emily Dickinson, and others "approximations" (*aproximaciones*). Jorge Luis Borges, from Argentina, translated into Spanish

William Faulkner's novel *The Wild Palms* (1939) in decidedly Borgesian, that is, un-Faulknerian, fashion. And Clarice Lispector, one of Brazil's most celebrated twentieth-century novelists, short story writers, and poets, was accused of "mistranslating" Edgar Allan Poe into Portuguese, especially "The Devil in the Belfry" (O Diablo no campanário), twisting Poe's ideas to make them integral to *el modernismo brazileiro*.

Toward the end of his lecture *"Lo judío* in Spanish-Language Literature," Gelman makes a stunning invitation in the form of "a wonderful dream." After discussing in detail how he had rewritten one of Yehuda Halevi's poems, "The Home of Love," he wondered if someone might use his own poem "as springboard, prolonging the writing initiated nine centuries ago, which echoes a poem of three centuries earlier." "Poetry is infinite," he said. "It allows us to feel infinite, names and people endlessly transformed by radiance, sealed by the desire to feed and be fed."

Part One

Quotes

(from *Citas* [1982])

Cita II (Santa Teresa de Ávila)

¿cómo es posible que viviendo
esta derrota/tu amistad
me cure el alma?/¿cómo
me consolás y amás/abriéndome

contra la áspera muerte/y decís
palabras herideras como leche
para comer como cordero/
poderoso de vos?

Quote II (Santa Teresa de Ávila)

how is it possible that amid this
defeat/your friendship
heals my soul?/how may you
console me/love me/ripping me up

against a merciless death/uttering
hurtful milky words
a lamb might eat/
almighty you?

Cita VIII (Santa Teresa de Ávila)

dolor de vos que no es como otros dueles/
mostrado a padecer grandes dolores/
sentado a tu sombrita me padezco/
oigo tu puño dándole a la sombra/

sombra de vos ardiendo contra el perro
de esta ventura como adiós/perfecta
consolación de vos/trabajo puro
donde mandás lo que quisieres/ancha

pena de vos como alma deleitosa
donde tus actos arden delicados/
o me escribís con vínculos de fuego/

atardecés en las campanas que
me gravemente tocan para alma
que te siguiera como perro/vos

Quote VIII (Santa Teresa de Ávila)

the pain you instill is like no other/
fated to bear great agony/
reclined under your gentle shadow I endure/
the sound of your beating fist on it/

your shadow burning against the doggish
venture like adieu/suitable
consolation of you/sheer labor
requesting to receive what you prefer/your

wide sorrow like a delectable soul
in which your acts are delicately consumed/
you write to me with gifts of fire/

your dusk in the bell rings
gravely touching me/making the soul
follow you like a dog/you

Cita XIX (Santa Teresa de Ávila)

y todo el cuerpo dolorido/frío/
el corazón enfriado como si
alma ya no tuviera/o respirar
para alentar/morir/dar vida al alma/

durar así días y días/como
padecimiento que arde de sí mismo/
y el alma en sus pasito por la de-
solación como vos/palabra tuya

venga de lo interior/no traiga pena/
no acobarde mi piel/no me murtée/
no me desastre/no me disemine/
o sea quereme vos/quereme/vos

Quote XIX (Santa Teresa de Ávila)

and the whole suffering body/cold/
a heart freezing as if the soul
no longer had it/or breathing
to encourage/die/grant life to the soul

lasting days and days/like
an illness consuming itself/
and the soul on its tight road
dissolving in you/your word

savages the inside/brings no pain/
doesn't coward my skin/doesn't killer me/
doesn't sour me/doesn't spread me/
love me then/love/me/you

Cita XXVI (Santa Teresa de Ávila)

ni cómo/ni por qué/ni qué querría/
alucinado amor cava mi alma/
apartado de sí como si fuera
a estar en vos/haciendo/deshaciendo/

y no se entiende lo que siente/y
no mueve pie/ni mano ni sombrita
menea en su quedar/parecer ido/
como salido/como adormizado/

o desmayadamente al pensamiento
trae pechos de unión/junta pedazos
yendo por sombras/silencioso como
lo ser que cesa alrededor de vos

Quote XXVI (Santa Teresa de Ávila)

not how/not why/nor what to wish/
imagined love caving my soul
departing from itself as if
to be in you/making/unmaking/

what is felt is not understood/
nor makes a move/a hand/a fragile shadow
swirling on its own/appearing gone/
as if departed/as if asleep/

passing out of mind
brings connecting breasts/gathering pieces
traveling through shadows/silent like
a being ceasing around you

Cita XXX (Santa Teresa de Ávila)

dolor que no es dolor/ya no/volando
fuera del ser/viniendo/yendosé/
ardiéndome sin acabar de arder/
apagándome como encendidísima

luz que mordiera mi deseo/pena
que no es puesta ni quitada/va
con tu sabor/o tempestad sabrosa
vuelta de otra región de vos/lucita

que no es melancolía/sino vos
trabajando por lo interior del alma/
labrándola/me sacundiendolá
para que suelte tuyas sus manzanas

Quote XXX (Santa Teresa de Ávila)

pain that isn't pain/no more/fleeing
from itself/back again/departing/
burning me with no consumption/
unburning me as if incited

light biting my desire/sorrow
not here or absent/enwrapping
your taste/your flavorful tempest
back from elsewhere/you/small light

without melancholy/but you
working inside my soul/
laboring it/shaking me from it
giving you its apples

Cita XXXI (Santa Teresa de Ávila)

¿me estoy que me deshago de deseo?/
¿y no sé qué pedir?/¿señora del
candor/que me pulís?/¿claro fueguito
que me arrancas la pena de esta entraña?/

¿la entraña con la pena me arrancás?/
¿me la quemás poquito?/¿qué no arda
ya toda en vos?/¿esperar todavía
debe?/¿cómo palabra que salís

chorreando sangre de la pobre alma?/
¿sangre como distancia/oscuridad/
a vos/de vos?/¿palabras que buscás
el sol de vos para sacarse el muere?/

¿palabra que sabés que no hay humana
consolación de vos?/¿qué podrá ser
esta quietud/este despierte/como
vida que alucinás con tu inocencia?

Quote XXXI (Santa Teresa de Ávila)

who am I unmaking my desire?/
do I not know what search is?/señora of
candor/polishing me?/crystal flame
ripping my sorrow from inside?/

do you tear the gut with the sorrow?/
do you burn inside me?/will it not
blister whole in you?/must it wait
again?/like a retiring word

spilling blood into a fragile soul?
blood like distance/darkness/
of you/from you?/to cleanse death
you search your word in the sun?/

word you know is not human
consolation of you?/what might this
quietude be/this awakening/
life imagining your innocence?

Cita XLV (Santa Teresa de Ávila)

¿memoria de mi ser?/¿humilde de uno?/
¿días sin descanso?/¿noches de trabajo?/
¿irse a la muerte/aunque se sepa/porque
se sabe?/¿miedo que quedaste atrás?/

¿ojos que pongo en vos?/¿palabras abiertas
de nada sirven?/¿hierro que marcás
mi corazón como yerra del alma?/
¿amor que grande en un solito no

puede estar?/¿viaja/cose de dolor
al amar?/¿sastre sentado a los pies/
sin hermanita que lo ayude?/¿triste?/
¿vida que hició/maltratándola mucho/

quemando amor con la sombra?/¿dura
vida que paga como encerramientos?/
¿arriba/abajo/a los costados/vos?/
¿jardines deleitosos?/¿fuentes?/¿vos?/

Quote XLV (Santa Teresa de Ávila)

memory of my being?/humbling one?
days without rest?/nights of labor?
embracing death/aware/might it be
known?/fear left behind?

eyes descending on you?/useless
open words?/metal stumping
the heart like an error of the soul?/
uncontainable lonesome love

suddenly allowed?/travel/sow your suffering
in love?/tailor your humility/
without a young sister to support you?/humbled?/
life impeded/mistreated/

bruising love against darkness?/suffering
life condemned to isolation?/
atop/below/on both sides/you?/
savory gardens?/fountains?/you?

Part Two

Commentaries

(from *Comentarios* [1982])

Comentario XXVIII (San Juan de la Cruz)

muchas maneras de recuerdos
suben de vos/oleajes íntimos/
o movimientos como mundos
girando a vos/en vos de vos/

tierra de vos que piso/ser
tendido como raicita
que tu recuerdo cubre contra
los animales de la noche

cuando a lo lejos crepitás
ajena en vos/de vos a vos/
o te soñás en mi recuerdo
que sueña recordandoté/

o conozco como recuerdo
tu rostro en cada rostro como
fulgor de vos/mirar de vos
donde me miro recordado

Commentary XXVIII (San Juan de la Cruz)

countless ways of remembering
ascend from you/intimate waves/
or movements like universes
spinning toward you/in you of you/

earth of you I step into/my self
stretched out as a small root
your memory protects against
the animals of night

when at a distance you rattle
alien to yourself/from you to you/
or dream yourself into my memory
that dreams remembering you/

or else I know your face
like memory in every face like
radiance from you/looking into
your eyes I see myself remembered

Comentario XLII (San Juan de la Cruz)

como tierna amorosa/vos/
tiernamente amorosamente
echás durezas/sequedades/
de mi país en tu país

donde llego desamargado
de la memoria a la sustancia/
o me sos lumbre/suavidad
levantada/graciosa mía/

cantora mía/en la mitad
de este destierro como arenas
del esperar al acabar/
mi vos/planeta de dulzura

Commentary XLII (San Juan de la Cruz)

as a tender lover/you/
lovingly tenderly
emit roughness/dryness/
from my country to yours

as I arrive unsoured
from memory to substance/
you are fire to me/ascendant
softness/gracious me/

chanter of mine/amid
this exile like sand dunes
waiting to end/
my you/planet of grace

Comentario XLIII (San Juan de la Cruz)

fuego que limpia en amor la alma
y la transforma en limpio amor/
echa llama además de arder
como palito que se extiende

hacia afuera de su madera/
y cada llama le alimenta
la voluntad de arder de vos
como palabra muy subida

volando alrededor de vos
como calor/como verdad/
o sea tiernísima de vos/
como torrente donde me almo

Commentary XLIII (San Juan de la Cruz)

fire cleansing the soul into love
transforming it in distilled love/
emitting a flame beyond burning
as a small expanding branch

onto the edge of the wood/
each flame feeding itself
with desire to burn in you
like elevated word

navigating around you
as heat/as truth/
as tender of you/
a torrent to love myself

Comentario XLVIII (Profeta Isaías)

suave luz alcanzada a ver/
olor olido una mitad/
como oído que te oyó una
vez que caías tan subida

en corazón de hombre como
flores abiertas a tu paz
de pastorita sola/vientre
haciendo sombras como amparos/

como mercedes contra el frío
de la furiosa/de la frente/
o como fiesta/resplandor
que inflama el aire/o almas tuyas

ardiendo alrededor de vos
como grandeza de cariño
donde el amor no se impacienta/
ni muere/ni recibe/ni

Commentary XLVIII (Prophet Isaiah)

soft light allowed to be seen/
smell smelled in half/
like an ear heard by you
once as you suddenly fell

in the heart of man like
open flowers in your peace
of lonesome shepherd/womb
granting shadow as shelter/

gifts against the cold
of the furious/in the forehead/
like fiesta/projection
inflaming the air/your souls

burning around you
in greatness of care
where love is not impatience/
or death/nor receive/nor

Comentario LVIII (Rey David)

como animal sediento que
busca las aguas/tierra mía
te busco/o alma de volar
para rodearte como vuelo/

o siquiera como palito
que tocara por una vez
la multitud de tu dulzura
barriéndome todas las sombras

Commentary LVIII (King David)

as the wild asses quench
their thirst/homeland I search
for you/you fix the branches
singing songs of the earth/

the trees drink their fill/
wrapped in splendor
you remove all darkness

Part Three

Com/positions

(from *Com/posiciones* [1986])

Exergue

JUAN GELMAN

I call the following poems com/positions because I have com/posed them, that is, I have placed my own things within texts written by great poets centuries ago. As is clear, I don't pretend to improve them. Shaken by their exilic vision, I have added—or changed, walked, offered—*that* which I have felt. As contemporaneous or company? Mine or theirs? Upside down? Inhabitants of the same condition?

At any rate, I am in dialogue with them. Just as they are with me, from the dust of their bones and the splendor of their words. I don't know what to celebrate the most: the beauty of their verses or the vital mouth that composed them. The two combine themselves to grant me a pass, surround my present, and gift me a future.

Such is the mystery of the human word. It proceeds, whatever the language, in the same flight between darkness and light, hence its shared substance: its light is dark, clear its darkness; with each language, each human group offers its voice for the flight to be possible; to prove, in each instant, its slowness, the way it bleeds out, how it works out.

To translate is inhuman: no language or face lets itself be translated. Untouched beauty must be left alone, supply another one to serve as company: only lost unity is to be found ahead.

That is what the Tower of Babel is about: not essential discord but partial science of the word. Reality has a thousand faces, each of them with its own voice, its own science, but also its own patience, so that the face and the word arise from the fear of trying to let them down. It is love that unites them, and time and the suffering, which, like patience, is at the end of the night where each word is a cold planet and the sun about to arrive.

Salmo I (Rey David)

¿dónde están mis murallas?
¿dónde la paz de mis muertos/semilla
diseminada en la memoria/o planta
que callada crecés?/¿está en vos?/
no te conozco/¿cómo conocerte?/
¿con qué nombre te puedo nombrar?/
¿cómo se llama en realidad la alondra?/
silencio sos de la palabra/
cuando no hablo soy en vos/
todo lo que me digo es silencio de vos/
pájaro que no vuela/buey
que no ara/mar que no mara/sol
que no camina por el cielo/¿sos
este abrigo que me desnuda en
tus muchas compasiones?/
¿me haces temblar de vos?/¿en vos?/
¿ciego de claridad/animal
que pace en tu paciencia?/

Psalm I (King David)

where are my walls?/
where will the dead find peace?/seed
disseminated in memory/or plant
growing quietly?/is it in you?/
I know not myself/how shall I know you?/
what name shall I use for you?/
what is the true name of the lark?/
you are the silence of words/
I am yours in silence/
all I say is silence of you/
bird unable to fly/ox
not plowing/sun
not passing through the sky/are you
this coat that undresses me in
your great compassions?/
making me tremble before you?/in you?/
blind with clarity/animal
gazing in your patience?/

Salmo II (Rey David)

no me dejes sin todo en todo/dame
algún mandato/acordate
del que cuenta las leyes de tu boca/
escribe/
los decretos de tu dulzura/pasa
lento por los caminos/
desterrado otra vez/siempre supe/
que conocerte era mi parte/
serte/existirte/abrime
la lengua de tu palabra/fundaste ya
mi corazón/y la alta noche/
tu apartamiento/tu bondad/

Psalm II (King David)

do not leave without much in much/grant me
some command/remember
he who counts the laws from your mouth/
write/
the decree of your sweetness/pass
slowly in your paths/
exiled once again/I always knew/
that knowing you was my role/
to be you/to exist in you/open myself
to the language of your word/you already founded
my heart/and the exalted night/
your isolation/your grace/

Salmo III (Rey David)

hablame como siempre/decí
que me querés/¿soy en tu vida
remordimiento?/sea tinieblas
mi vida/no noche
donde te pueda respirar/¿qué tengo
sino mi fe en mañana?/
mi corazón no piensa/
sangro en tu luz de ayer/
linar de mi consuelo/
estoy siempre más lejos
de mí/rumbo sin vos/
sólo mi pensamiento
te oye a mi lado/palomita
que en el aire escribís adiós adiós/
vuelo errante/
clausura de mis huesos/

Psalm III (King David)

speak to me as always/tell me
you love me/am I remorse
in your life?/let my life
be darkness/not night
where I might breathe you/what do I own
if not my faith in tomorrow?/
my heart thinks not/
it bleeds in your past light/
coin of consolation/
I am always far
from myself/on the path without you/
only my thought
listens at your side/little dove
spelling goodbye goodbye in the air/
errant flight/
closure from my bones/

El buey (Profeta Amós)

la congoja me abraza/¿estoy uncido
a vos/para que are
mi soledad/la ropa
raída de mi alma?/oh leche
de tus pies/mojan el mundo/
mi corazón/no desisten
de su inocencia/cosen
las furias de tu ausencia/
ya des/dicha/fiadora
de mi pobreza/o desnudez/

The Ox (Prophet Amos)

grief enwraps me/am I tied
to you?/for me to plow
my solitude?/the ragged
clothes of my soul?/oh milk
of your feet/my heart/
wets the world/won't
surrender its innocence/sow
the rages of your absence/
made un/joyed/guarantor
of my humility/or nakedness

El llamado (Profeta Ezequiel)

¿gemís como quien tiene quebrantado los lomos?/
¿rodillas de agua?/¿gemís
en la amargura de tu corazón?/¿por qué
gemís?/¿por quién?/almita

dormida al fondo de tu infancia/
despertá/sacudite la noche/
como los pájaros se sacuden las gotas de la noche/
mirá el heraldo gris del alba/

su espada gris/almita
presa de la esperanza/
recibí su poder/
dale tu amor/

The Calling (Prophet Ezekiel)

do you scream and howl like one with disjointed loins?/
knees of water?/you howl
so that the heart faints and tumbling blocks abound?/why
howl?/for whom?/tender little soul

stay whetted at the end of childhood/
wake up/shake off the night/
as birds shaking off the drops of night/
embrace the gray herald of dawn/

its gray spear/tender little soul/
prisoner of hope/
accept your wrath/
grant it your love/

El fénix (Job)

fui soberbio/creí
que eras una página en blanco
como tu alma/confundí
tu bondad con candor/tu candor
con desvío del mundo/escribí
líneas equivocadas/palabras/
en la noche obsedida de mí/pero no
fui ojos para el ciego/pies al rengo/
me creí revestido de justicia/pensaba
"pereceré en mi nido y como el fénix
redoblaré mis días"/pero fui
insensato y grosero/equivoqué
mi camino hacia vos/
roto de muro/forzada la puerta/
las penas se arrojaron sobre mí/
se empecinan en mí/que ya soy nada/
te fuiste como el viento/vos/lo que más amé/
mis huesos/parentela
del polvo y la ceniza/
claman por vos y no me oís/
estoy en tu presencia y no me ves/
corto mis pasos hacia vos/
pacto no verte con mi vista/
y tengo un solo paradero: la muerte/

The Phoenix (Job)

I was arrogant/I believed
you were a blank page
like your soul/I mistook
your kindness with candor/your candor
with rejecting the world/I wrote
the wrong lines/words/
in the night obsessed with me/but I had
no eyes for the blind/less for the lame/
I believed myself above justice/I thought
"In my nest I shall breathe my last, and my days
will abound like the sand"/but I was
senseless and unkind/I mistook
my path toward you/
the wall in ruins/the door forced/
sorrow accumulated in me/
stubborn/I was nothing/
you departed like the wind/you/what I loved the most/
my bones/kinship
between dust and ash/
they clamor for you and you won't hear me/
I am in your presence and you won't see me/
shorten my steps toward you/
I agree not to see you with my sight/
and have only one destiny: death/

Árboles (Rollos del Mar Muerto)

de creador a criatura/
voy por tu amor/me alzás/abrís tu mano/
aunque no sabo aún hacer la casa
que deseás contra el frío/o las furias
del pobre corazón/te llevo
como sello en mi lengua/amor/
fuerte como la muerte/pasión/
cierta como la tumba/centro que
convierte en dulces pechos tu palabra/
tu vientre/o alma al sol/

Trees (Dead Sea Scrolls)

from creator to creature/
I seek your love/you raise me/open your hand/
I don't yet know how to build a house
you want against the cold/or the rage
of a humble heart/I carry you
like a seal in my tongue/love/
implacable as death/passion/
unquestionable like the tomb/a center
turning your word into sweet breasts/
your womb/or soul to the sun/

Lo que vendrá (Rollos del Mar Muerto)

el que no anduvo su pasado/
no lo clavó/no lo comió/no sabe
el misterio que va a venir/
nunca puso su vida/para
el misterio que va a venir/la pena
desaparecerá/un gran humo
se alzará de la sed/de la hambre/de
la injusticia/la soledad/arderán
como leños/los astros
se tranquilizarán/
y todo será verde/
como el misterio del dolor/
como tus pechos blancos
bajo el manzano/

What Will Come (Dead Sea Scrolls)

he who has not gone over his past/
nor dug it up/nor eaten eat it/knows not
the mystery of what will come/
has never offered up his life/to
the mystery of what will come/sorrow
will vanish/a great cloud of smoke
will rise up out of thirst/out of hunger/out of
injustice/solitude/the logs
will burn on a fire/the planets
will settle down/
and all will be green/
like the mystery of pain/
like your white breasts
beneath the apple tree/

Maitines (Himno Hekhalot)

por vos comienza la alabanza/
empieza la canción/
nacen la alegría y el júbilo/
¡oh bella/como nave
que navega/cielo que ciela como
techo de cámara nupcial!/tus pechos
anulan votos/revocan decretos/
tranquilizan la furia/convocan
a la ternura/llaman al amor/
¿cómo vivir con tantos resplandores?/
¿tanto deleite/miedo/
de tenerte/perderte?/¿por
qué a veces reís/otras llorás?/
esperarte es un niño
bajo la lluvia/¡oh rostro de
la majestad/hermoso/rostro
de llama/rostro ardiendo entre novios!/
quien te vio sabe que es el otro/
ya rompe el alba/y
se calla la creación/
oye el silencio
de todas tus criaturas/

Morning Prayer (Hekhalot Hymn)

the song of praise begins in you/
the song begins/
joy and jubilation are born/
oh beautiful/like a sailing
ship/sky skying
like ceiling of a nuptial chamber!/your breasts
cancel votes/revoke decrees/
apace the fury/convene
tenderness/congregate love/
how to live with such splendor?/
such delight/fear/
of having you/losing you?/why
do you at times smile/others cry?/
waiting for you is like becoming
a child under the rain/oh face
of majesty/beautiful/face
of fire/burning face among lovers!/
whoever saw you knows they are the other/
dawn arrives/and
creation is muted/
witnessing the silence
of all your creatures/

Ojalá (Himno Hekhalot)

milagro/poder/maravilla
flotando/sin moverse/clavija
de violín que dirige la danza del mundo/
su perfección/esta hora de amor/
ave séptima/cielo/
revoloteando/sin moverse/
coronada de las criaturas que
creás/llena de fuerza/de temblor/de noche/
de reverencia/de abandono/
me balanceás/no me movés
de tu gracia/tu vestidura
está bordada de palabras
que nadie ha de mirar/quien lee
cae ciego de luz/
allá ardiera/bien mío/
me consumiera en tu grandeza/
bajara a vos en mí
subiendo a vos/

Let Us Hope (Hekhalot Hymn)

miracle/power/floating
wonder/motionless/violin
peg of the loom fixing the world's course/
its perfection/this hour of love/
seventh bird/heaven/
fluttering/motionless/
crown made of the creatures
you created/full of force/of tremor/of night/
of reverence/of abandon/
you shake me/not from
your grace/your clothing
embroidered with words
no one shall see/whoever reads
is blinded by light/
burning distant/my love/
I shall be consumed in your greatness/
lowering you in me/
ascending to you/

El momento (Samuel Hanagid)

me dijo que me alegre/
"Dios te dio ya 50 años sobre el mundo"/ella me dijo/y
no sabe/ni sospecha que/
bajo las telas de mi corazón/
no hay diferencia entre los días que viví
y los días viejísimos en que Noé vivió/
en el mundo sólo tengo esta hora/
este ahora que soy/
muestra su rostro y
como una nube/pasa

The Moment (Samuel Hanagid)

she asked me to rejoice/
"for God has brought you to your fiftieth year in the world!"/she said to me/and
has no inkling/or even imagines that/
under the tissues of my heart/
there's no difference between the days I lived
and the ancient days when Noah lived/
in the world this hour alone is mine/
this now that I am/
showing its face and
like a cloud/passing by

Momentos de la batalla de Alfuente (Samuel Hanagid)

el enemigo alzó sus tiendas en la cuesta del monte/
nosotros en el desfiladero/
las lanzas fulguraron al sol/
y estalló el día del odio/de cólera/de furia/
los hombres procuraban los premios de la muerte/
el día fue una oscura niebla/
el sol nocturno/así mi corazón/
la tierra se tambaleó como un borracho/
los caballos saltaban
como víboras súbitas del nido/
ese viento mortal de jabalinas/
golpeaban las flechas como lluvia contra nuestros escudos/
las espadas contrarias encendían diamantes en la noche/
la sangre de los hombres por el suelo/
como la sangre del cordero a los pies del altar/
mis hombres que reían del vivir/del morir/
una corona es cada herida en su rostro/
oh jóvenes leones/
morir/creyeron/es guardar la fe/
vivir sin fe/pensaron/es prohibido

Scenes from the Battle of Alfuente (Samuel Hanagid)

the enemy pitched his tents on the mountainside/
we pitched ours in the pass/
swords shone under the sun/
and the day of anger burst/of jealousy/of rage
men uncovered the awards of death/
it was a day of darkness and thick fog/
the nocturnal sun was as black as my heart/
the earth rocked on its pillars as if it were drunk/
horses lunged back and forth
like vipers darting out of their nest/
the mortal wind of lances/
arrows pelted us as if our shields were sieves/
the opposing swords turned on like diamonds in the night/
the blood of men flowed upon the ground/
like the blood of rams on the corners of the altar/
my men scorned their lives/preferring death/
a crown is each injury in their face/
oh young lions/
to die/they believed/is to keep the faith/
to live without faith/they thought/is forbidden/

La derrota (Samuel Hanagid)

calló la guerra/el derrotado
mira sus ruinas/su alma/
su escudo roto/
la soberbia del vencedor/los astros
lejos de él/
arden como los días de batalla
en que desenvainó su corazón/
con los trapos de la memoria limpia
la espada que empuñó/
la pasión que se oxida de noche/

The Defeat (Samuel Hanagid)

war was silent/the defeated
ponders his ruins/his soul/
his broken shield/
the victor's pride/stars
distant from him/
burn like the days of battle
when he unsheathed his heart/
with the rags of the cleansed memory
the sword he wielded/
passion rusting at night/

Invitación (Samuel Hanagid)

daría mi vida por
la que arpas y flautas despertaran
en mitad de la noche/
y me viera
con la copa en la mano/
y dijera
"tu vino está en mi boca"/
y la luna parecía una C
con tinta de oro escrita
en las paredes de la noche/

Invitation (Samuel Hanagid)

I would give my life so that
harps and flutes may awaken
in the middle of night/
to let her see me
with a goblet in my hand/
and I would say
"your wine is in my mouth"/
and the moon resembled a C
written in gold ink
in the walls of night/

Sí (Samuel Hanagid)

subía la luna/le dijiste
"¿cómo vas a brillar
mi rostro ardiente?"/
tenías razón/

contra tu rostro/la
luna es una esmeralda
en la palma
de una muchacha negra/

Yes (Samuel Hanagid)

the moon raised/you told her
"how will you shine
over my burning face?"/
you were right

against its face/
the moon is an emerald
in the palm
of a black girl/

El vino (Samuel Hanagid)

rojo al ojo/dulzor al bebedor/
su cuerpo arde en España/
su aroma toca la India/
languidece en la jarra/espera
desatarte la boca/iluminarte el paladar/
celebrar un misterio en tu cabeza/
el desdichado que aún tiene corazón/
sangre en el corazón/mezclada
con lágrimas/levanta
la jarra/prohíbe penas
con la sangre de un pueblo de racimos/
gira la jarra/va
de una mano al calor de otra mano/
como si cada amigo
puliera un rostro del diamante/

Wine (Samuel Hanagid)

red in the eye/sweetness to whoever drinks/
his body burns in Spain/
his aroma touches India/
languishing in the jar/the moth
awaits disaster/to illuminate your palate/
celebrating a mystery in your head/
the miserable still with a heart/
blood in the heart/mixed
with tears/raise
the jar/forbidding sorrows
with the blood of a people made of bunches/
the jar travels/
goes from the warmth of one hand to another/
as if each friend
polished one of the diamond's faces/

Al saber que mi enemigo murió (Samuel Hanagid)

yo soñé con tu muerte/después
soñé en tu muerte/¡ibn abi musa:
mis dos sueños cumpliste!/
¿mutilaron tu cuerpo/arrastraron
tu ya cadáver por las calles?/
mis pies danzan y mis manos aplauden/
me corroboro con manzanas/con vino
baño mi paladar/mi vieja llaga/
¿te torturaron/te
destrozaron el alma con
las dos miserias de la carne rota?/
hoy no leeré los lamentos/
hoy leeré el cantar de los cantares/
la súbita aparición de la esposa/
bella como la luna/
brillante como el sol/terrible
como ejército en orden de batalla/
me aparta de tu rostro/oscuro/hundiéndose/
bebo en las tazas de la esposa/
sus pechos de licor inextinguible/
beso el trigo que crece en su vientre
rodeado de azucenas/mientras vos
ibn abi musa/
visitas el hedor de la tumba/
te enterás de la noche del pozo/
sólo un silbido de serpientes
acompaña tu viaje a las cenizas/
yo estoy aquí/me perfumo/me ciño
las ropas de la fiesta/pienso en
la fortaleza en ruinas
donde una vez pensé en los generales/
los soldados/los constructores/los
destructores/los esclavos/los amos/
los poderosos/los mendigos/
las plañideras/los recién casados/

los padres y los hijos/
que alguna vez se alojaron encima
de la tierra/y se alojan ahora
en la tierra/pasaron
de la alta luz al polvo/como vos/
ibn abi musa/
como yo pasaré/
como el odio que nos ató/
con furias/sus terrores/

On Learning of My Enemy's Death (Samuel Hanagid)

I dreamt your death/later on
dreamt at your death/ibn abi musa:
you fulfilled my two dreams!/
did they mutilate your body/did they
drag your fresh corpse through the streets?/
my feet dance and my hands clap/
I celebrate with apples/with wine
I rinse the roof of my mouth/my old wound/
did they torture you/destroy
your soul with
the scraps of the mangled flesh?/
today I will not read the lamentations/
today I will read the song of songs/
the bride's sudden appearance/
beautiful like the moon/
radiant as the sun/terrifying
as an army ready to battle/
I am removed from your face/blurred/sinking/
I drink in your bride's cups/
her breasts of inextinguishable liqueur/
I kiss the wheat growing in her womb
surrounded by white lilies/while you/
ibn abi musa/
visit the stench of the tomb/
you discover the night in the pit/
you have only the hissing of serpents
for company in your journey to ashes/
I am here/I put on perfume/change
into festive clothes/recalling
the fortress in ruins
where I once thought about the generals/
soldiers/builders/
ravishers/slaves/masters/
the powerful/beggars/
hired mourners/the newly wed/

parents and offspring/
who once inhabited
the earth/now housed
under the ground/they passed
from elevated light to dust/like you/
ibn abi musa/
like I will pass/
like the hatred that bound us/
its rages/its terrors/

La puerta (Salomón ibn Gabirol)

abrí la puerta/amor mío/
levantá/abrí la puerta/
tengo el alma pegada al paladar
temblando de terror/

el jabalí del monte me pisoteó/
el asno salvaje me persiguió/
en esta medianoche del exilio
soy yo mismo una bestia/

The Door (Solomon ibn Gabirol)

open the gate/my love/
arise/open the gate/
my soul is dismayed
shaken with terror/

I was trampled by the wild boar/
Then pursued by the wild ass/
on this midnight of exile/
I am like a beast/

La pérdida (Salomón ibn Gabirol)

me dejó/se fue al cielo/
la de bella garganta envuelta en un collar/
tiene labios dulcísimos/
pero ella es amarga/

sacaba espadas de sus ojos/
lanzas que afila para matar a los hombres sin suerte/
sus ojos hacen señas/
está llena de ansias/como venado sediento/

su ceja/o arco/o arcoíris/
recuerda el pacto con Noé/la señal que el diluvio acabó/
si tenés sed/
ella ordena a sus nubes inundar tu corazón de cristales/

The Loss (Solomon ibn Gabirol)

she left me/went up to heaven/
she whose neck is so lovely with its ornaments/
her lips are sweetest/
but she is bitter/

swords are unsheathed from the scabbards of her eyes/
lances are burnished to kill unlucky men/
her eyes beckon to me/
she is full of longing/as a thirsty deer/

her eyebrow/or arch/or rainbow/
calls to mind Noah's covenant/a signal that the deluge is over/
when you thirst/
she orders her clouds to flood your heart with crystals/

Los testigos (Salomón ibn Gabirol)

dijeron a la joven del cabello que besa sus mejillas
"¿cómo puede el mediodía de oro besar al alba rosada?"/
"vano es lo bello/desilusiona la ilusión"/ella dijo/
pero no estaba hablando de ella/
sus mejillas no mienten/declaran
que los actos de Dios son insondables/

The Witnesses (Solomon ibn Gabirol)

they said to the young woman with hair kissing her cheeks
"how can yellow moon enfold the rosy dawn?"/
"beauty is vain/charm is delusion"/she said/
but do not hold it against him/
her cheeks bear true witness/declare
the acts of God are unfathomable/

Oración (Yehuda Halevi)

tu hiciste nido de mi amor/y mi amor
vive donde vivís/los enemigos
me atormentan/que sean/sea su ira/
mientras no encuentre mi camino hacia vos/
mis huesos tiemblan sosteniendo a un extraño/
al extranjero de tu piel/
así sea/
mientras no absuelvas mi dolor/
me sudes/me redimas/
me rescate de mí/

Prayer (Yehuda Halevi)

you became my nest of love/and my love
lives where you live/the enemies
tormented me/let them be/let your ire be/
as long as I don't find my path to you/
my bones tremble embracing a stranger/
the foreigner of his own skin/
let it be/
as long as you don't absolve my pain/
seat me/redeem me/
rescue me from myself/

Lavar (Yehuda Halevi)

en mis lágrimas lavo las ropas del amor/
las tiendo al sol de tu belleza/
no necesitan fuente: están mis ojos/
ni mañana: solo tu resplandor/

To Wash (Yehuda Halevi)

in my tears I rinse the clothes of love/
drying them in the sun of your beauty/
no fountain is needed: I have my eyes/
nor tomorrow: only your glow/

Canción (Yehuda Halevi)

¿por qué/vos/bella/no enviás mensajeros
al que te ama/al que es pena de vos?/
¿acaso no sabés que el tiempo es nada para mí?/
¿qué el tiempo sólo empieza con vos?/
ya seremos pedazos/ahora/
déjame ver tu rostro una vez más/
no sé nada de mi corazón/no
sé si se detuvo en mi pecho/
o vaga alrededor de vos/
te pido/por amor al amor/
que recuerdes tus días de deseo/
como recuerdo yo tus noches de pasión/
un mar de lágrimas mueve su oleaje entre nosotros/
y no puedo cruzarlo para llegar a vos/
si te acercaras a la orilla
las aguas se abrirán a tus pies/
oh/después que yo muera/
dale a mi corazón permiso/y oiga
las campanitas de oro
que vuelan en el vuelo de tu falda/
ojalá viva yo
hasta juntar la mirra y el incienso
que sembraron tus pies en este invierno/
no puedo oír tu voz/
pero en lo hondo de mi corazón/
en su guarida/
oigo tus pasos/

Song (Yehuda Halevi)

why/you/beautiful/don't you send messengers
to the one who loves you/the one who suffers for you?/
don't you know time means nothing to me?/
time begins with you?/
we will be but fragments/now/
let me behold your face once more/
I know nothing of my heart/I know not
whether it has stopped in my breast/
or wandered looking for you/
I beg/for the sake of love in love/
remember your days of want/
as I won't forget your nights of passion/
a sea of tears breaks between us/
I cannot cross to reach you/
if you won't approach the shore
the waters will part at your feet/
oh/once I die/
grant my heart leave/allow it
to listen to those small golden bells
tinkle in the sweep of your dress/
allow me to live
until myrrh and incense unite
your feet have sown this winter/
though your voice I cannot hear/
from the depth of my heart/
in its hideout/
I listen to your steps/

El país de la paloma (Yehuda Halevi)

oh/corazón absorto/vos soñás/
ardés en furias/despertate ahora/
avanzá en la luz de su presencia/
levántate y andá/un astro se alza
desde el fondo de un pozo desolado/
es de tu propio pozo que ella asciende
y se muestra y se oculta/vos quemás
tu sangre en rabias y consentimientos/
y quien se compadece/sino vos/
de tus exilios/tus pedazos/

The Country of the Dove (Yehuda Halevi)

oh/contrite heart/you dream/
burning in fury/wake up now/
advance in the light of its presence/
rise up and walk/a star ascends
from the bottom of a desolate well/
it is from your own well that it ascends
manifesting itself and hiding out/you burn
your blood in anger and consent/
who shall be moved/if not you/
after your exiles/your fragments/

Decir (Yehuda Halevi)

qué es este cuerpo mío/interminable
arde/tus pechos
mueven en dos la noche/
y él muerovive en tu entender/
come los libros de la sombra/
es tu no conocida hermosura/
la que se esconde en tu hermosura/
sol de este exilio/que
seguís/girás/eternidades/
hasta la clara oscuridad/

To Say (Yehuda Halevi)

what is this body of mine/burning
without end/your breasts
divide the night in two/
and he lives-in-death in your wisdom/
like the books of shadow/
it is your unknown beauty/
hiding behind your beauty/
sun of this exile/you
follow/turn/eternities/
until the clearest darkness/

El ciego (Yehuda Halevi)

quise olvidarte/pero
mi olvido no te olvida/
puse losas heladas sobre mi corazón
y él late a tu compás/
soy dos/
uno come/procura/el otro
cava mis huesos/grita
lo amado/amado está/

The Blind Man (Yehuda Halevi)

I wished to forget you/but
my forgetfulness doesn't forget/
I placed frozen slabs on my heart
and it palpitates at your rhythm/
I am divided/
one eats/procures/the other
digs my bones/screams
of what is loved/and is loved/

El expulsado (Yehuda al-Harizi)

me echaron de palacio/
no me importó/
me desterraron de mi tierra/
caminé por la tierra/
me deportaron de mi lengua/
ella me acompañó
me apartaste de vos/y
se me apagan los huesos/
me abrasan llamas vivas/
estoy expulsado de mí/

Expelled (Yehuda al-Harizi)

they expelled me from the palace/
I didn't care/
they exiled me from my land/
I wandered the earth/
they deported me from my language/
but it accompanied me
you separated me from yourself/and
my bones are extinguished/
I am embraced by living flames/
I am cut off from myself/

La mano (Eliezer ben Jonon)

tu corazón/o dulce aviso/
pueblo de separados/palabra
que no pronunciarás/silencio
de tu bondad/auxilio
contra la ira que consume
este palito/este bajar al polvo/
sin subir a tu gracia/
este fuego que arde en tu resplandor
y no sabe limpiarse/asemejarse
a tu vosear en mí/no estés lejos/
custodiá mi inocencia/mis aguas muchas/
el pudor de mis huesos/
la insolencia/o desgracia/
de mudo corazón/

The Hand (Eliezer ben Jonon)

your heart/or sweet warning/
people of fracture/word
you will not pronounce/silence
in your kindness/help
against the ire consuming
this little stick/this descent to dust/
incapable of rising to your grace/
this fire burning in your glow
knows not how to be cleansing/resembling
your sameness in me/don't distance yourself/
protect my innocence/my thunderous waters/
the modesty of my bones/
insolence/or disgrace/
of the muted heart/

El camino (Eliezer ben Jonon)

deleite mío/estás bañada
de gracia/o ríos donde mojo
mis furias/abrazadas
por tu hermosura/¡no recuerdas
tu pueblo ni la casa de tu padre!/
¡bella sos caminando
de la colina clara a tu dulzura/
de tu temblor a mi temblor!/

The Road (Eliezer ben Jonon)

delight of mine/you are bathed
in grace/or rivers where I wet
my rages/embraced
by your beauty/don't remember
your people nor your father's house!/
beautiful as you walk
from the clear hill to your sweetness/
from your shake to my shake!/

La cuestión (Eliezer ben Jonon)

tu candor/piedra viva/
alimento de mí/
rostro de vuelo/y ese
rubor de fuego/como espada/
o delantal contra la furia/cabeza
que agaché/deslumbré/
en tus hierbas/varona/
donde no hay mal/ni bien/
sino delicia/noche
pegada al paladar/

The Question (Eliezer ben Jonon)

your candor/living stone/
nourishment of me/
face of light/and such
blush of fire/like a sword/
or apron against the rage/head
I bent down/dazzled/
in your grass/female
where no evil is found/nor good/
but delight/night
stuck to the palate/

Rostros (Eliezer ben Jonon)

este camino/¿es solo para mí?/
¿esta pasión?/¿este cuchillo?/
soledad/
si tenés hambre/¿te daré de comer?/
si tenés sed/¿te daré de beber?/
estos clavos que clavan/¿son para mí?/
¿son rostros de tu rostro/amada?/
vos/
que no podés iluminar/
dame otra vez la noche/las tinieblas
de tu cuerpoalma/o luz/o pechos/que
me confirman para que me deshaga/
de mí/de mis pedazos/¿qué es
esta disolución en vos/no pena/
no castigo/no cárcel/transparencia
que va de la nada y vuelve amor?

Faces (Eliezer ben Jonon)

this road/is it only for me?/
this passion?/this dagger?/
solitude/
if you are hungry/will I feed you?/
if thirsty/will I give you something to drink?/
these nails that nail/are they for me?/
are they faces of your face/beloved?/
you/
able to be enlightened/
grant me once again the night/the darkness
of your palmbody/or light/or breasts/
asking me to vanish/
from me/of my fragments/what
is this dissolution in you/no sorrow/
no punishment/no prison/transparency
traveling to nothingness and returning as love?/

El juicio (Joseph Tsarfati)

esa gracia que el tiempo vio crecer en tu frente/
el tiempo habrá de cosecharla/no la devolverá/
y el alto trono que creías alto y tuyo por siempre/
el tiempo al foso abajará/
y el dolor con que me ataste en tus horas de triunfo/
con su hacha y su cuchillo el tiempo cortará/
el tiempo abaja/el tiempo alza/
de la tierra de nadie el exiliado partirá

The Judgment (Joseph Tsarfati)

that grace time saw growing in your forehead/
time will reap/it will not give back/
and the high throne you believed so high and yours forever/
time will lower it into the grave/
and the bonds you tied me down with in your hour of victory/
with its ax and knife time severs/
time lowers it all/time rises up/
from the land of no one the exiled will depart

Dónde (Isaac Luria)

¿en qué tinieblas te envolvés?/
no hablo con vos/no me oís hablar/
no te respiro/no te veo/me forjan
los martillazos de tu ausencia/
siempre te amaré/siempre
mis versos doloridos de vos
diré en la soledad/como si fueras
fruta secretamente habida/
ciega bajo la falda
de una niña/perdida en su memoria/
huyendo/
triste de su rubor/

Where (Isaac Luria)

in what distress do you shield me?/
I don't speak with you/you don't hear me/
I don't breathe your inside/I don't see you/your
absence forges me with blows/
I will love you forever/always
I will cry out my verses about you
in solitude/as if you were
a secretly obtained fruit/
blind under a girl's
dress/lost in her memory/
fleeing/
unhappy in its blush/

Allí (Isaac Luria)

en la sombra/en el día/
en la noche que ningún grito de
gozo interrumpe/en
la bondad que sirvieran

como vino/como belleza que
araste el mundo/niño
que pregunta por qué no morí
en dulce claustro/en suave olvido/

en el suelo que el tigre
pisa/pesa en su luz sin ojos/en
tu cabeza/caballo que

como púrpura/o brillo/
en la úlcera del tiempo/
en todos mis caminos/

There (Isaac Luria)

in the darkness/in the day/
in the night no joyful howl
interrupts/in
the kindness served

as wine/like beauty
plowing the world/child
asking why I didn't die
in sweet cloister/in tender oblivion/

on the floor the tiger
steps on/eyeless while weighing in its light/in
your crown/horse

seemingly purple/or glowing/
in the ulcer of time/
in all my paths/

El huérfano (Isaac Luria)

¿qué pasa?/¿por qué cada día
me perseguís como a enemigo?/
¿me tendés trampas?/¿me acosas?/
¿clavás tu fiebre en mi carne?/
mi alma soñó en seguirte/
en quedarse a la sombra de tu mano/
quieta/salvada de dolor
por tu mano/pero me hacés llorar
ante el guardián nocturno/me llamás
nada y en nada me convierto/
yo/el destinado a la dulzura
de tus palabras/soy el huérfano/
mirá que pronto dormiré en el polvo/
cuando me busques no me encontrarás/
¿a quién arrojarás tu anzuelo entonces/
le engancharás el paladar/
lo tirarás a su destino?/
si me acuesto/pregunto
cuándo la autora llegará/
si me levanto/pregunto
cuándo la noche llegará/
apuro al tiempo para verte/
estoy exiliado de mí/
como el Creador de todo lo creado/

The Orphan (Isaac Luria)

what is the matter? why do you
always pursue me as an enemy?/
you set hidden traps for me?/you catch me in my own snare?/
nail your fever to my flesh?/
my soul dreamed of following you/
in sheltering in the shade of your hand/
still/saved under the shadow
by your hand/but eyes awoke
before the night watch/you call me
nothing and I become nothing/
I/who is destined to the sweetness
of your words/I am an orphan/
witness how fast I shall sleep in the dust/
you will not find me when you look for me/
who will then throw your bait?/
hooking his palate/
you will push him into his fate?/
if I lie down/I ask
when shall dawn come/
if I rise up/I ask
when shall night arrive/
I hurry time to see you/
exiled from myself/
like the Creator of all creation/

Part Four

Letter to My Mother

(from *Carta a mi madre* [1989])

Carta a mi madre

A Teodora

recibí tu carta 20 días después de tu muerte y
cinco minutos después de saber que habías muerto
/una carta que el cansancio, decías, te
interrumpió/te habían visto bien por entonces/
aguda como siempre/activa a los 85 años de
edad pese a las tres operaciones contra el cáncer
que finalmente te llevó/

¿te llevó el cáncer?/¿no mi última carta?/la
leíste, respondiste, moriste/¿adivinaste que me
preparaba a volver?/yo entraría
a tu cuarto y no lo ibas a admitir/y nos
besábamos/nos abrazamos y lloramos/y nos
volvemos a besar/a nombrar/y estamos juntos/
no en estos fierros duros/

vos/que contuviste tu muerte tanto tiempo/¿por
qué no me esperaste un poco más?/¿temías por
mi vida?/¿me habrás cuidado de ese modo?/
¿jamás crecí para tu ser?/¿alguna parte de tu
cuerpo siguió vivida de mi infancia?/¿por eso
me expulsaste de tu morir?/¿Cómo antes de vos?
/¿por mi carta?/¿intuiste?/

nos escribimos poco en estos años de exilio/
también es cierto que antes hablamos poco/
desde muy chico, el creado por vos se rebeló de
vos/de tu amor tan estricto/así comí rabia y
tristeza/nunca me pusiste la mano encima para
pegar/pegabas con tu alma/extrañamente
éramos juntos/

no sé cómo es que mueras/me sos/estás
desordenada de mi memoria/de cuando yo fui
niño y de pronto muy grande/y no alcanzo a fijar

tus rostros en un rostro/tus rostros en un aire/
una calor/un aguas/tengo gestos de vos que son
en vos/¿o no es así?/¿imagino?/¿o quiero
imaginar?/¿recuerdo?/¿qué sangres te repito?/
¿en qué mirada mía vos mirás?/nos separamos
muchas veces/

nací con 5,5 kilos de peso/estuviste 36 horas en
la cama dura del hospital hasta sacarme al
mundo/me tuviste todo el tiempo que tu cuerpo
me pudo contener/¿estabas bien conmigo
adentro?/¿no te fui dando arrebatos,
palpitaciones, golpes, miedos, odios,
servidumbres?/¿estábamos bien, juntos así, yo
en vos nadando a ciegas?/¿qué entonces me
decías con fuerza silenciosa que siempre fue
después?/debo haber sido muy feliz adentro
tuyo/habré querido no salir nunca de vos/me
expulsaste y lo expulsado te expulsó/

¿esos son los fantasmas que me persigo hoy
mismo/a mi edad ya/como cuando nadaba en tu
agua?/¿de allí me viene esta ceguera, la lentitud
con que me entero, como si no quisiera, como si
lo importante siga siendo la oscuridad que me
abajó tu vientre o casa?/¿la tiniebla de grande
suavidad?/¿dónde el lejano brillo no castiga con
mundo piedra ni dolor?/¿es vida con los ojos
cerrados?/¿por eso escribo versos?/¿para volver
al vientre donde toda palabra va a nacer?/¿por
hilo tenue?/la poesía ¿es simulacro de vos?/¿tus
penas y tus goces?/¿te destruís conmigo como
palabra en la palabra?/¿por eso escribo versos?/
¿te destruyo así pues?/¿nunca me nacerás?/¿las
palabras son estas cenizas de adunarnos?/

nos separaste muchas veces/¿eran separaciones?
/¿formas para encontrarse como primera vez?/
¿ese imposible nos hacía chocar?/¿eso me
reprochabas en el fondo?/¿por eso eras tan triste
algunas tardes?/tu tristeza me era insoportable/
a veces quise morirme de eso todavía/¿ya tenía
mi pedazo de vida para ocuparme de él?/¿cómo
animal cualquiera?/¿ya soy triste por eso?/¿por
tu tristeza ofende la injusticia/escándalo del
mundo?/

siempre supiste lo que hay entre nosotros y nunca
me dijiste/¿por culpa mía?/¿te reproché todo el
tiempo que me expulsaras de vos?/¿ése es mi
exilio verdadero?/¿nos reprochamos ese amor
que se buscaba por separaciones?/¿encendió
hogueras para aprender la lejanía?/¿cada
desencontrarnos fue la prueba del encuentro
anterior?/¿así marcaste el infinito?/

¿qué olvido es paz?/¿por qué de todos tus rostros
vivos recuerdo con tanta precisión únicamente
una fotografía?/Odessa, 1915, tenés 18 años,
estudiás medicina, no hay de comer/pero a tus
mejillas habían subido dos manzanas (así me lo
dijiste) (árbol del hambre que da frutas)/esas
manzanas ¿tenían rojos del fuego del pogrom que
te tocaba?/¿a los 5 años?/¿tu madre sacando de
la casa en llamas a varios hermanitos?/¿y muerta
a tu hermanita?/¿con todo eso/por todo eso/
contra/me querés?/¿me pedías que fuera tu
hermanita?/¿así me diste esa mujer, dentro/
fuera de mí?/¿qué es esta herencia, madre/esa
fotografía en tus 18 años hermosos/con tu largo
cabello negriazul como noche del alma/partida
en dos/este vestido acampanado marcándote los
pechos/las dos amigas reclinadas a tus pies/tu

mirada hacia mí para que sepa que te amo
irremediablemente?/

¿así viaja el amor/de ser a antes de ser?/¿de ser
a sido en tu belleza?/¿viajó de vos a mí?/¿viaja
ahora/morida?/nada podemos preguntar sino
este amor que todo el tiempo nos golpeó/con su
unidad irrepetible/¿para que nos olvidemos el
dolor?/¿los dos niñitos del mercado de Ravelo
con una gallinita en los brazos, ofreciendo barato
y con gestos de madre, casi recién salidos de sus
madres?/¿por qué te apareciste en el mercado
boliviano?/¿en cada pena estás?/apagabas el sol
para dormirme/

¿podés quitarme vida?/¿ni quitártela yo?/
¿castigabas por eso?/desciendo de tus pechos/tu
implacable exigencia del viejo amor que nos
tuvimos en las navegaciones de tu vientre/
siempre conmigo fuiste doble/te hacía falta y me
echaste de vos/¿para aprender a sernos otros?/
cada mucho nos dabas un momento de paz:
entonces me dejabas peinarte lentamente y te ibas
en mí y yo era tu amante y más/¿tu padre?/¿ese
rabino o santo?/¿qué amabas?/¿más que a mí?/
¿me perseguías porque no supe parecerme a él?/
¿y cómo iba a parecerme?/¿no me querías otro?/
¿lejos de ese dolor?/¿por qué tan vivo está lo
que no fue?/¿nunca junté pedazos tuyos?/¿cada
recuerdo se consume en su llama?/¿eso es la
memoria?/¿suma y no síntesis?/¿ramas y nunca
árbol?/¿pie sin ojo/mano sin hora?/¿nunca?/
¿saliva que no moja?/¿así atan los cordones del
alma?/¿vos sos dolor, miedo al dolor?/

¿qué fue lo separado?/¿mi dedo de escribir en tu
sangre?/¿mi serte de no serte?/y vos, ¿no eras

el otro?/¿cuántas veces miraste las llamas del
pogrom mientras yo te crecía, entraste al bosque
donde cantaba el ruiseñor que nunca oí, jugaste
con el que nunca fui?/nacimos junto a dos
puertos distintos/conocemos las diferencias de la
sal/vos y yo hicieran un mar desconocido con
dos sales/

me hiciste otro/no sigas castigándome por eso/
¿te sigo castigando por eso?/¿y sin embargo/y
cuándo/y yo tu sido?/¿vos en yo/vos de yo?/
¿y que podemos ya cambiar?/¿pudimos cambiar
algo alguna vez?/¿nunca saldé las hambres del
abuelo?/los ojos claros del retrato que presidía tu
cuarto/¿qué puede el verdadero amor cambiar?/
¿o nos es de tal modo que nos empuja a ser sí
mismos?/¿para uno en el otro?/¿resonando en
las partes de la noche?/¿cómo dos piedras contra
el cielo?/¿pájaro y árbol?/cuando se posa el
pájaro en el árbol, ¿quién es vuelo, quién tierra?/
¿quién baja a oscuridad?/¿quién sube a luz?/
¿qué goce pasa a llaga?/¿te llevo en llaga viva?/
¿para que nos atemos otra vez?/¿este sufrido
amor?/

me hiciste dos/uno murió contuyo/el resto es el
que soy?/¿y dónde la cuerpalma umbilical?/
¿dónde navega conteniéndonos?/madre harta de
tumba: yo te recibo/yo te existo/
¿trato de amor hay en la sombra?/¿ya volveré a
peinarte el dulce pelo/espesura donde mi mano
queda?/¿pensativa en tu aroma?/¿gracia
cuajada en lenta parecida?/¿me quisiste
imposiblemente?/¿así me confirmaste en el
furor?/¿puerto de tardes inclinadas al que volvías
tantas veces?/¿dónde navegarás ahora sino en mí/
contra mí?/¿puerto solo?/bella de cada mar en
mi cabeza/llaga de espumas/alma/

no sé qué daño es éste/tu soledad que arde/
dame la rabia de tus huesos que yo los meceré/
vos me acunaste yo te ahueso/¿quién podrá
desmadrar al desterrado?/tiempo que no volvés/
mares que te arrancaste de la espalda/tu leche
constelada de cielos que no vi/leche llena de
sed/tus pechos que callan/paciencias/
caballitos que el pasado maneó/llenos de estepa
detenida/rota por mi avidez de vos/así me
alzaste/me abajaste/me amaste sin piedad/
pañal feroz de tu ternura/

¿o yo fui tu cansancio?/¿te reproché que me
expulsaras?/¿nos ata ese reproche hondísimo/
que nunca amor pudo encontrar?/¿no me quisiste
mar y navegar lejos de vos?/¿tiempo hecho de
vos?/¿no me quisiste acaso otro cuando me
concebías?/¿otra unción de esa unidad?/¿ama
total de tus dos sangres?/¿te das cuenta del
miedo que nos hiciste, madre?/¿de tu poder/tu
claridad?/

¿qué cuentas pago todavía?/¿qué acreedores
desconozco?/necesito recorrer una a una tus
penas para saber quién soy/quién fui cuando nos
separamos por la carne/dolorosa del animal que
diste a luz/sierva mía/ciega de mi servidumbre
de tu sierva/pero esas maravillas donde me
hijaste y te amadré/tu cercana distancia/

¿me ponías a veces delantales de fierro?/¿me
besabas a veces con pasión?/¿y qué pasión había
en tu pasión?/¿no podrís cesar en tu morir para
decirme?/¿no te querés interrumpir?/entraste
tanto en tu desaparecer?/¿volvés al desamparo de
mí?/¿tan duro era mi amor?/¿te di un alma y
con otra te echaba a mi intemperie?/¿no pudiste
morirvivirme en suave claustro/no darme de

nacer?/mi nacer, ¿te habrá apagado ganas de
matarme?/¿eso me perdonabas y no me
perdonabas?/¿así peleaste con tus sombras?/
¿así me hiciste sombra tuya de otro cuerpo, me
diste tu pezón/campo violeta/donde pacía un
temblor?/¿techo contra el terror?/¿única tela de
la paz?/¿no la tejíamos los dos?/¿en mañanas
cayendo sobre el patio donde jamás hubo otra
gloria?/¿blancuras que de vos subían?/¿rocíos
de tu sangre al puro sol?/¿lluvia de abajo
interminable?/¿yo fui animal de lluvia?/¿te
ensucié pechos con mi boca?/¿me diste a veces
leche amarga?/¿te olvidás de las veces que no
quise comer de vos?/¿qué te venía entonces de la
entraña del alma?/esos jugos, ¿no me atardecen
fiero?/¿y vos creés que estás muriendo?/¿antes
que muera yo?/¿y se apaguen los gestos que
escribiste en mi cuerpo?/¿las dichas que
imprimiste?/¿en mi querer a las mujeres?/
¿prolongándote en ellas?/¿que de vos me
tuvieran y alejaran?/

¿qué yo habré sido para vos?/¿cómo me habrás
sufrido cuando salí de vos?/no saberte, ¿no es
ni saber de vos?/yo no sé por qué cielos giraste/
sé que giran en mí/nada pudiste finalmente
ahorrarme/no soy sin vos sino de vos/no me
reproches eso/todavía me entibia el blancor de tu
nuca/y mis besos allí/siervos de esa armonía/
¿cuántas veces se detuvo allí el mundo?/¿cuántas
veces cesaste la injusticia allí/madre?/¿cuántas
veces el mundo endureció tu leche?/¿la que me
abraza/la que me rechaza/la que te pide
explicaciones?/¿ya solísima/y tarde/y tan
temprano?/

y esta tarde/¿no está llena de usted?/¿de veces
que me amó?/la voz que canta al fondo de la

calle/¿no es su voz?/¿temblor de vientre juntos
todavía?/¿qué es este duro amor/tan suave y
tuyo/lluvia de tu fuego/fuego de tu madera/llama
escrita en el fuego con tu huesito último/ardor de
pie en la noche?/¿alta??/¿qué gritás en mi alma?
/pero no me gritás/tu paladar entrado a tiendas
de la sombra siento frío/¿cuántas veces sentiste
mis fríos?/¿me habrás mirado extrañada de vos?
/¿no te fui acaso el peor de los monstruos?/¿el
creado por vos?/¿y cómo hiciste para amarme?/
¿ese trabajo dabas de comer contra tu propia
oscuridad?/y cuando abrí la boca, ¿no gritaste?/
¿no se asustó tu lengua de mi lengua?/¿no hubo
un jardín de espanto en tu saliva?/¿qué sembré/
cultivé/regué con mi tu sangre?/¿y qué te habré
morido al darme la luz?/¿y la profundidad de mis
desastres?/¿y nuestro encuentro inacabado/ya
nunca/ya jamás/ya para siempre?/¿y pedregal
de vos a vos donde sangraron mis rodillas?/
¿cuándo junto a mi cuna llorabas tantas cosas/y
mi fiebre y la fiebre de tu salvaje juventud?/

así mezclaste mis huesitos con tu eternidad/tus
besos eran suaves en noches que me dejaste solo
con el terror del mundo/¿me buscabas también
así?/¿hermanos en el miedo me quisiste?/¿en
un pañal de espanto?/¿o me parece que fue así?/
¿dónde se hunde esta mano/dónde acaba?/
¿escribís, mano, para que sepa yo?/¿y sabés más
que yo?/tocaste el pecho de mi madre cuando fui
animalito/conociste calores que no recuerdo ya/
bodas que no conoceré/¿qué subtierra de la
memorias arás?/¿soy planta que no ve sus raíces?
/¿ve la planta raíces?/¿ve cielos/empujada?/
¿cómo vos, madre, me empujás?/mi mano, ¿es
más con vos que mismo yo?/¿siente tu leche o
lunas de noche en mí perdida?/

¿y mi boca?/¿cuánta alma te chupó?/¿te fue
fiesta mi boca alguna vez?/¿y mis pies?/¿me
mirabas los pies para verme el camino?/¿y tu
ternura entonces?/¿era tu viaje hacia mi viaje?/
¿fuiste rodeada de temor amoroso?/¿del caminar
por mí?/¿por qué nunca supimos arreglar el
dentrofuera que nos ata?/¿al afuerino de tu
cuerpo?/tu leche seca moja mi alma/¿ahora la
soy?/¿me es?/¿cuáles son los trabajos del
pájaro que nunca me nombrás?/¿el que nos
volaría juntos?/¿ala yo/vuelo vos?/me
obligaste a ser otro y tu perdón me muerde las
cenizas/¿acaso yo podría prolongar tu belleza?/
¿sin convertirla en cuerpo de dolor/lengua
exiliada de tu nuca??/¿y cuánto amé la ausencia
de tu nuca para que no doliera?/¿y que te
devolviera?/¿a dulzura posible en este mundo?/
¿conocida que no puedo nombrar?/¿vientre que
nadie puede repetir?/¿lleno de maravilla, de gran
desolación?/¿pasó a río deshecho por mis pies?/
¿tan duro tu olvidar?/poderosa, ¿soy el que vos
morís?/¿ceñido de tu nombre?/¿por qué te abrís
y te cerrás?/¿por qué brilla tu rostro en doble
sangre todavía?/

pasé por vos a la hermosura del día/por mí pasás
a la honda noche/con los ojos sacados porque ya
nada había que ver/sino ese fino ruido que
deshace lo que te hice sufrir/ahora que estás
quieta/
¿y cómo es nuestro amor/éste?/
envolverán con un jacinto la mesa de los panes/
pero ninguno
me hablará/estoy atado a tu suavísima/doy de
comer a tu animal más ciego/
¿a quién das tregua/vos?/
están ya blancos todos tus vestidos/
las sábanas me aplastan y no puedo dormir/te

odiás en mi completamente/se crecieron la mirra
y el incienso que sembraste en mi vez/dejá que
te perfumen/acompañen tu gracia/mi alma
calce tu transcurrir a nada/
todavía recojo azucenas que habrás dejado aquí
para que mire el doble rostro de tu amor/
mecer tu cuna/lavar tus pañales/para que no me
dejes nunca más/
sin avisar/sin pedirme permiso/
aullabas cuando te separé de mí/
ya no nos perdonemos/

Letter to My Mother

To Teodora

I received your letter 20 days after your death and
five minutes after finding out you had died
/a letter that weariness, you said,
interrupted you/they had found you sound around then/
sharp as ever/active at the age of 85
in spite of three operations for the cancer
that finally took you away/

did cancer do it?/not my last letter?/you
read it, answered it, died/did you guess
I was preparing myself to go back?/I would enter
your room and you wouldn't admit it/and we
would kiss/we hugged each other and cried/and we
would kiss again/say each other's name/be together again/
not in these hard irons/

you/who held off your death for so long/why
couldn't you wait for me a bit longer?/did you fear
for my life?/did you protect me that way?/
did I never grow up before your eyes?/did
some part of your body go on living off my childhood?/is
that why you expelled me from your dying?/as you did before
from your being?/because of my letter?/did you intuit it?/

we seldom wrote each other in those years of exile/
it's also true that we spoke little to each other before then/
from early on, the one created by you rebelled against
you/against your strict love/that's how I digested my share of rage and
sadness/you never laid a hand on me/
you whipped me with your soul/strangely
we were close/

I don't know how you die/you're me/you are
disorganized in my memory/from when I was
a child and suddenly much older/I cannot fix

your faces in a face/your faces in a wind/
a warmth/waters/I have gestures from you that are
in you/is that not so?/am I imagining??/or am I wanting
to imagine?/do I remember?/what bloods do I repeat to you?/
through what sight of mine do you see?/we got apart
many times/

I was born weighing 5.5 kilos/you were 36 hours
in a hard hospital bed until I came out into
the world/did you have me all the time your body
could contain me?/were you comfortable
with me inside?/didn't I give you fits,
palpitations, kicks, fears, hates,
servitudes?/were you and I well together, I
inside you swimming blindly?/what did you
tell me then with the silent strength you always had
later on?/I must have been very happy inside
you/I must have not wanted to come out of you/you
expelled me and the expelled expelled you/

are those the ghosts I haunt myself with
today/at my age now/as when I swam in your
water?/is that where this blindness, this slowness
comes from, so slow finding things out, as if I didn't want to,
as if what is important is the darkness your
womb or home reduced me to?/darkness with its infinite
softness?/where the distant brightness doesn't punish with
a stoned world or pain?/is it life when we have our
eyes closed?/is that why I write poems?/to return
to the womb where every word is about to be born?/by
a tenuous thread?/poetry, is it a simulacrum of you?/your
sorrows and your joys?/do you destroy yourself with me like
a word inside the word?/is that why I write verses?/
do I destroy you this way?/will you never be born of me?/are
words these ashes that make us one?/

you separated us countless times/were they separations?
/ways of meeting each other for the first time?/
was that impossibility making us clash?/was that why you
reproached me in the end?/is that why you were so sad
some afternoons?/your sadness was unbearable to me/
at times I wanted to die because of it/did I already have
my piece of life to occupy myself?/like another
animal?/am I sad as a result?/does your sadness offend
injustice/scandal in the world?

you always knew what exists between us but never
told me/was it my fault?/did I blame you all the
time for expelling me from you?/is that
my real exile?/did we blame each other for that love
we sought through separations?/did it set
bonfires to light up distance?/was every
non-encounter proof of the last encounter?/
is that how you mapped infinity?/

what oblivion is ever peace?/of all your living
faces why do I recall with such precision only
one photograph?/Odessa, 1915, you were 18 years old,
studying medicine, there was nothing to eat/but two
apples had risen to your cheeks (that's what
you told me) (the tree of hunger that yields fruit)/did those
apples have red tints from the fire in the pogrom that
you touched?/at the age of 5?/your mother getting several
siblings from the burning house?/and your young sister
dead?/with all that/because of that/
against that/do you love me?/did you want me to be your
young sister?/is that why you gave me this woman/inside/
and outside me?/what is this heritage, mother/that
photograph of you at your beautiful 18 years of age/with long
hair as blue-black as the night of the soul/parted
in the middle/that flared dress emphasizing your
breasts/the two friends reclined at your feet/your
eyes looking at me so I would know I love you
irrevocably?/

is this how love travels?/from being to before being?/
from being to having been in your beauty?/did it travel
from you to me?/does it travel now/dead?/we can
no longer ask anything but this love beating us all the time/
with its unrepeatable unity/so that we don't forget
suffering?/the two children from the market in Ravelo
with a tiny hen in their arms, selling cheap and
with motherly gestures, almost newly born
from their own mothers?/why did you show up in
the Bolivian market?/are you in each sorrow?/
you turn off the sun to put me to sleep/

can you take life away from me?/can I take it from you?/
is that why you punish me?/I come from your breasts/your
implacable demand of the old love we
had in the navigations of your womb/
you were always duplicitous with me/you missed me and you
expelled me/so that we would learn how to be others?/
every so often you gave us a moment of peace:
then you would allow me to slowly comb your hair and you
departed from and in me and I was your lover and more/
your father?/that rabbi or saint?/you loved him?/more than me?/
did you come after me because I didn't know how to be like him?/
and how could I be like him?/didn't you want me to be someone else?/
far from that suffering?/why is alive that which never was?/
did I never gather pieces of you?/does every reminiscence
vanish in its own flame?/is that what memory is?/addition
but not synthesis?/branches but never tree?/foot without eye,
hand without hour?/never?/unwet saliva?/is this how
the threads of the soul knot us together?/are you pain, fear of pain?/

what was it that was separated?/my finger scribbling in your
soul?/my being in you without being?/and you, weren't you
the other?/how many times did you look at the flames from the
pogrom while I was gestating in you, entering the forest
where I never heard the mockingbird sing, where you played
with the one I never was?/we were born together in two
separate ports/we know the differences of salt/

you and I could make an unknown sea with
two salts/

you made me another/don't go on punishing me for that/
do I continue punishing you with that?/and nevertheless/and
when/I was your past?/you in me/you from me?/
can we still change something?/can we ever
change anything?/did I ever account for my grandfather's
hungers?/the clear eyes in the portrait presiding in your
room/what can true love change?/
or is it such that it pushes us to be who we are?/
one in the other?/echoing in
the parts of the night?/like two stones against
the sky?/birds and tree?/when the bird stands still
on the tree, who is in flight, who is land?/
who descends to darkness?/who ascends to light?/
what joy becomes sore?/do I carry you in a fresh sore?/
so that we tie ourselves together again?/this suffering
love?/

you made me two/one died with you/the other
is who I am/and where is the umbilical bodysoul?/
where does it travel containing us?/mother tired of
tomb: I write to you/I exist in you/

are there ways to treat love inside the shadow?/will I ever
comb your sweet hair again/thickness/where my hand
remains?/thoughtful in your aroma?/curdled
grace in slow resemblance?/did you love me
impossibly?/is that how you confirmed me in
furor?/a port of bent afternoons to which you returned
time and again?/where will you sail now if not in me/
against me?/lonesome port?/beautiful from each sea in
my head/sore made of foam/soul/

I don't know what injury is this/your burning solitude/
give me the anger of your bones for me to rock them/
you cradled me and I bone you/who will

unmother the banished?/time to come no more/
sea you tore away from your back/your constellated
milk made of skies I never saw/milk full of
thirst/your breasts were silent/patiences/
horses the past twirled/full of interrupted
steppe/broken because of my avidity of you/that is how
you elevated me/by bringing me down/you loved me
without piety/fierce encampment of your tenderness/

or was I your exhaustion?/did I reproach you for
expelling me?/does that profound reproach tie us together/
one no love was able to find?/did you want me
to become the sea and sail away from you?/time made of
you?/did you perhaps not want me to be someone else
when you conceived me?/another union of that unit?/total
owner of your two bloods?/are you aware of the
fright you turned us into, mother?/of your power/your
clarity?/

what balances do I go on holding?/what creditors
do I not know?/I must go over each one of your
sorrows to know who I am/who I was when we
separated from each other in the flesh/painful of the animal
you gave birth to/my servant/blind of my servitude
of your servant/but those marvels where you
birthed me and I made you mother/your close distance/

did you at times dress me in metal aprons?/did you
at times kiss me passionately?/and what passion was there
in your passion?/could you cease in your death to
tell me?/would you want to be interrupted?/did you
enter so deeply as to disappear?/might you return to the helplessness
of me?/was my love so strong?/did I give you a soul and
with another one I threw you out into the open air?/could you not
dielive in soft cloister/not make me
be born?/my birth, did it turn off in you the desire to
kill me?/did you forgive and not forgive me?/
is that how you fought with your shadows?/

is that how you turned me into a shadow of you
from another body, you gave me your nipple/violet field/
where a tremor lurked?/sealing against terror?/sole fabric
of peace?/didn't we both sow it?/in mornings
descending over the patio where there was never another
glory?/whiteness that ascended from you?/dew
made of your blood exposed to the sun?/interminable rain
from below?/was I a rain animal?/did I get your breasts
with my mouth?/did you at times feed me
sour milk?/do you forget the times I didn't want to
eat from you?/what did you then feel in the
gut of your soul?/those juices, do they not make me
rest fiercely/and do you think you're dying?/before
I myself die?/so that the gestures you
inscribed in my body?/the joys you imprinted?/
in my love of women?/prolonging yourself in them?/
so they would at once have me and distance me through you?/

what must I have been for you?/how must you have
suffered me when I came out from you?/not knowing you, isn't that
my knowledge of you?/I don't know in what skies you wandered/
I know they wander in me/in the end you didn't save
anything for me/I am not you but of you/don't
reproach me that/you still warm the whiteness of your
nape/and my kisses there/servants to that harmony/
how many times did the world stop there?/how
many times did you cease the injustice there/mother?/how many
times did the world harden your milk/the one
embracing me/the one rejecting me/the one asking me
for explanations?/are you now alone/and late/and very
early?/

and this afternoon/isn't it full of you?/of the times
you loved me?/the voice singing at the end of the
street/isn't it your voice?/tremor of the womb still
together?/what is this hard love/so soft and
yours/rain of your fire/fire of your wood/flame
written on the fire with your last little bone/ardor

standing at night?/high?/what are you screaming in my soul?
/but you don't scream at me/your palate entered into shadow
tents I feel cold/how often did you feel
my colds?/would you have looked at me with estrangement?
/was I perhaps not the worst of monsters for you?/the one
created by you?/how did you do to love me?/
did you feed that labor against your
darkness?/and when I opened my mouth, did you scream at me?/
did your tongue not get frightened in my tongue?/was there
no garden of horror in your saliva?/what did I plant/
did I cultivate your blood with me?/and what might I have
bitten when you gave birth to me?/and the depth of my
disasters?/and our unfinished encounter/already
never/already ever/already forever?/and stone road
of you to you where my knees bled?/
what many things did you cry near my crib/and
my fever/and the fever of your savaged youth?/

this is how my tiny bones with your eternity/your
kisses were soft in the nights you left me alone
with the horror of the world/were you looking for me also
that way?/did you love me like siblings in fear?/in
a diaper of horror?/or do I believe it was that way?/
where does this hand sink/where does it end?/
are you writing, hand, so I learn?/do you know
more than I do?/did you caress my mother's breast when I was
a little animal/did you know warmth I no longer recall/
weddings I will not know/what underworld of
memory do you plough through?/am I a plant unable
to see its roots?/do plants see their roots?/do they witness
the sky/pushed?/how do you, mother, push me?/my hand, does it belong
more to you than to me?/do you feel your milk or
night moons in my loss?/

and my mouth?/how much soul did it suck from you?/was
my mouth a party for you at any point?/and my feet?/did
you look at my feet to understand my path?/and your
tenderness then?/was your journey toward my journey?/

were you surrounded by loving fear?/from walking
for me?/why didn't we ever learn to fix the
insideout we are tied with?/the outside of your
body?/your dried milk wets my soul/am I it
now?/it is me?/what are the bird's travails you
never named for me?/the one that would
fly us together?/am I a wing/you a flight?/you
forced me to be someone else and your pardon bites
the ashes in me/could I have prolonged your beauty?/
without turning it into a body of pain/exiled
language from your nape?/and how much did I love the absence
of your nape so it wouldn't hurt?/and what would it have
returned to you?/would it have returned to you a possible sweetness
in this world?/the known one I cannot name?/womb no one
can repeat?/full of wonder, great desolation?/did it become
an undone river through my feet?/is your forgetting
so harsh?/mighty, am I the one you're dying?/tied
to your name?/why do you open up and close down?/why
does your face shine in double blood/still?/

through you I came to the beauty of the day/through me you go
deep into the night/with your eyes withdrawn because
there was nothing more to see/except that fine sound that
undoes all I made you suffer/now that you're
motionless/
and what's this love of ours like?/now?/
with hyacinth they'll cover the table once filled with breads/
but no one
will talk to you/I'm tied down to your softness/I
feed your blindest animal/
who do you grant respite to/you?/
all your dresses are now white/
the sheets smother me and I can't sleep/you
completely hate yourself in me/myrrh
and incense you planted in my time have grown/allow them
to cover you with scent/to accompany your grace/allow my soul
to prepare your passing into nothingness/
I still harvest lilies you might have left here

to look at the double face of your love/
to rock your cradle/to wash your dippers/so you can
never leave me again/
without warning/without asking permission/
you howled when I separated you from me/
let's never forgive each other again/

Part Five

Lo judío and Spanish-Language Literature

(1992)

Lo judío and Spanish-Language Literature

A complex topic. To what degree do Jewish writers in Spanish create Jewish literature, or in any language other than Yiddish and Hebrew? Each language has its own worldview, inherited—supported, one might say—through generations of speakers, a language that says *perro* and not *chien, dog* and not *sabaka*. What each word in a language contains within itself, silences and statements and silences again, is tied to a constellation of meanings shared with all the words in that language, connected with a blue fire that tenuously illuminates its night, a fire that suddenly shines or fades away, never to be extinguished altogether, constantly undulating, like liquid metal, its fulgor announcing the firmness of its foundation, the great whole of that language.

The mother tongue is the one that connects us to a vision of the word built across time and to those who share that language and that vision. What is in that vision is called the verbal unconscious, made of an infinite number of anonymous speeches. That unconscious shapes us. My belief is that the only true Jewish writers—I'm talking about literature—are the ones who have written, and still write, in Yiddish or Hebrew (and the special case of *sefardí*). There are dimensions in a writer that are indiscriminately juxtaposed: language, on one side, the language in which one writes; and on the other, nationality or religion. For example, Kavafis: is he an Egyptian or a Greek poet? Born in Alexandria, Egypt, in his seventy years he only visited Greece a couple of times, only a month each time. Two months in total. But one cannot say Kavafis was an Egyptian poet. He was a great Greek poet.

Something along the same lines happens with writers born in the former French colonies, who opt to write in French. Take the case of Tahar Ben Jelloun, awarded the Goncourt Prize, an award for excellence in the French language, among other things. Or the cases of Aimé Césaire, from Martinique, and of the Haitian writer René Depestre. Someone said of the former that "he had written in the language of white people, burdened by Africa's imagination." Much of Haiti is in the poems and novels of Depestre, but his French expressions leave off the page the peculiarity of Creole, the Haitian identity forged in the language of Haiti and from which Haiti emanates.

Language, as I said, is much more than a worldview; it has an unconscious, a depository made over centuries. It also has a matrix sustaining us in which we are contained, one still feeding us as we feed it after we are thrown out of the womb. We travel from the womb to the mother tongue, from the womb to another womb that is spiritual, which won't abandon us until our death. Don't we all feel, when we speak, and especially when we write, the irrigations of that matrix shaping our mouth, its obscurities, waters, and navigations, its secret and circular beat, the realization that behind the translucent wall of nothingness there is another world, a world we barely glimpse without ever touching, whose distant closeness touches us like an absent present speaking to us, making us be spoken to by that "otherness"—world, language, mystery, or hole—in whose eye the infinite passes through? Is "otherness" God for San Juan de la Cruz? Is "otherness" the *zot* in King David's psalms? Is "otherness," in definite terms, everything the Spanish language silences as it speaks? The unconscious of our language is inhabited by *lo judío*, all that is Jewish capable of finding a place in it.

That all literature is born of language, and is a child and a mother of language, is obvious and doesn't require demonstration. The same might be said of all the texts in Spanish: they constitute Spanish-language literature. But that doesn't mean that more specific dimensions fail to intervene, attempting to enter the Spanish language. This is the case of Rodolfo Walsh's Irish Catholic ingredients, at least in some of his texts. Or the Jewish dimension of Alberto Gerchunoff and César Tiempo. Or of Borges, who, as Saúl Sosnowski explains in his exemplary book *Borges y la Cábala*, nurtured a deep love for Kabbalah [spelled Cábala in Spanish]. The word *leikaj*, honey-sweetened cake, baked by Jews during Rosh Hashanah, doesn't have the same flavor in Yiddish or Spanish.

The Jewish dimension certainly palpitates in the writing of all of us present today. Why negate that Shabbat candles and Passover meals have left an imprint in me, the imprint that, according to Plotinus, a formless thing leaves in the soul? I can deny even less that I was born in Argentina and that Argentine society and the culture of a certain class have left deep marks in me, which means I belong to the great nation of the Spanish language, its visions, sounds, silences, its continents and islands, the ways it explodes into hate and love. We are all spoken through that language, and what is extraordinary is that other languages, the languages of exile, flow into the great river that is the language spoken by Argentinians, widening it, adding tributaries that descend from the Po River, the Dnieper River, the Vistula River, changing the color of its waters with the slime carried over by language and deposited in the depth of its adventure, a never-ending adventure.

But what is likely to be the Jewish dimension of the Spanish language? Or maybe one should ask about the "Spanish" worldview, which is perhaps universal. This theme is vast and ought to elicit the attention of philologists, aestheticists, literary critics, and, why not, theologians.

Let me explain why theologians. We all know Santa Teresa de Ávila's dwellings, *Las moradas*: there are seven on the road to ascendance toward God. In the hymns called Hekhalot—precisely, *hekhalot* in Hebrew means palaces— there are exactly seven palaces the soul must pass through as it journeys toward the superior heaven in order to reach God. According to Gershom Scholem, these hymns are the "unsurpassable expression of Hebrew hymnology." The point is that Santa Teresa wrote her dwellings at the end of the sixteenth century—in 1577—and the shaping of the Hekhalot, which are still preserved, dates to the third and fourth centuries CE, although some go back to the second century, and we also know that Jewish mysticism was born in the first century before Christ, in Palestine and Babylon.

The road taken by this mystical vision in Hebrew is complex, and so are its influence in eighth- and ninth-century Sufism. The vision returns to the Jews through Sufism in later centuries, and eventually it leaves a mark on Spanish mysticism. It is a fact that Santa Teresa was the granddaughter of Juan Sánchez, a converso Jew reconciled in Toledo in 1485, who suffered because of his Jewish condition. Julio Caro Baroja, in his book *La sociedad criptojudía en la corte de Felipe IV* [Crypto-Jewish Society in the Court of Felipe IV, 1963], tells that, for a time, Santa Teresa's grandfather was seen "in infamous processions, with a Sanbenito," the dress code identifying Jews, just like the Star of David did five centuries later under the Nazis. Santa Teresa was named after her maternal great-grandmother, Teresa Sánchez, also a conversa. The very name Teresa is a converso name, an amalgam of the name Esther. It isn't difficult to imagine a path from the Hekhalot hymns to Santa Teresa's dwellings. Caro Baroja argues that "the history of Castile's old conversos is written in fragments; it deserves a dynamic investigation making us see how far its influence reaches, not only in economic and social trends, but also spiritually, in certain mental patterns not exactly studied by 'Golden Age' scholars." José Ángel Valente comments further: "Mental habits, spiritual currents—actually, one of the least attended research fields, I believe, is Jewish spirituality in Spain." Indeed, Spanish scholars have always been inclined to accept Arabic, rather than Jewish, influence, which explains a certain current of anti-Semitism, of anti-Judaism, coloring the so-called objectivity of these types of studies, even though the Jewish name Teresa-Esther is in the pantheon of Catholic saints.

Santa Teresa says in *Camino de la perfección* [Road to Perfection, 1583]: "Pretend that inside you there is a palace of enormous value, its entire edifice made of gold and jewelry . . . and it is you who gives the palace its value . . . and the palace is inhabited by the Great King . . . in his valuable throne." Valente adds: "Here the reformist nun uses two symbolic elements—palace and throne—to structure the ecstatic vision described in the Hekhalot."

I underline *ecstatic*: we are talking about a mystical experience. Yet poetry is also an ecstatic experience, the experience of "getting out of oneself" until nothing stops us from speaking or silencing the "otherness" that turns us into spoken or silenced creatures, meaning that language goes through us unimpeded, carrying us along in its never-ending voyages. This is the experience, for instance, of Moisés Cordovero, possibly the most important Kabbalist of all time, born at the beginning of the sixteenth century in northern Galilee. In that period, this region was of supreme religious importance for Jews, especially Safed, where Cordovero was born and where sages and rabbis had settled after being expelled from Spain in 1492. Today we celebrate the quincentennial of the "encounter" of Europe and the Americas, or better, the clash of cultures. In truth, 1492 was the year of the great *desencuentro*, disencounter of cultures in Spain, when the Catholic monarchs finally tore to pieces a splendid three-part cultural tapestry, an Arabic, Jewish, and Christian knot of outstanding historical riches.

At the time, it was customary to practice "expulsions" in Safed. Moisés Cordovero, age twenty-five, in the company of his teacher Solomon Alkabetz and of a number of study partners, embarked on voluntary "expulsions," known as *guiruchin* [Hebrew for divorce, rejection]. These consisted of walking on the Galilee roads in search of the divine presence, also expelled and in a wandering state. (That idea of an exiled and wandering God is extraordinary, in harmony with that of another Kabbalist, Isaac Luria, who taught that the first great exile was God himself, expelled from everything He had created.) The walkers would talk about Kabbalah and visit their teachers' tombs in search of inspiration. Rabbi Cordovero describes the practice as follows: "In 1547, while 'expelled,' to consecrate ourselves to the study of Torah, on the road with the holy Rabbi Solomon ben Alkabetz Halevi—may his memory be blessed and protected—spontaneously, without reflection, words would come to us in such ways that only those having gone through the adventure many times would understand." Cordovero includes this account in *Sefer Guiruchin*, a book he wrote between ages twenty-four and twenty-nine. He mentions the revelations achieved during those walks, thanks to a practice, he says, and I quote him directly, where "words are pronounced by themselves."

Today we talk of intertextuality. This is another complex theme, from Julia Kristeva to the present, and even from [Mikhail] Bakhtin to the present, with explanations going back and forth without end. I won't pretend to immerse myself in this theoretical forest, but I would like to mention an old technique of the Hebrew poets of the al-Andalus school in the thirteenth century, a practice linked to what [Jean] Ricardou has defined as "restricted intertextuality." Dunash ben Labrat, founder of the school, his acerbic rival Menahem ibn Saruk, and other poet colleagues developed, among other things, a peculiar technique: the insertion, in their poems, of biblical texts skillfully interwoven, from a short phrase to a complete verse. The biblical quote could be textual, lightly altered, or elliptical; it could create a vast range of effects in meaning, at times contradicting the original. In the poems by [Yehuda] al-Harizi, for instance, the effect is openly comical: a complete poem might consist of the articulation of the biblical quote, or, in his case, an alluvion of quotes and allusions might become, in its metaphorical effect, the very substance of the poem.

Perhaps it is pertinent to quote Borges here. "What is good," he said, "belongs to no one, not even to the other, but to language and tradition." Or let me recall Ezra Pound, who in his essay "The Serious Artist" (1913) stated that "the so-called major poets have most of them given their own gift but the peculiar term 'major' is rather a gift to them from Chronos. I mean that they have been born upon the stroke of their hour and that it has been given them to heap together and arrange and harmonize the results of many men's labour. This very faculty for amalgamation is a part of their genius and it is, in a way, a sort of modesty, a sort of unselfishness. They have not wished for property. The men from whom Dante borrowed are remembered as much for the fact that he did borrow as for their own compositions. At the same time he gave of his own, and no mere compiler and classifier of other men's discoveries is given the name of 'major poet' for more than a season. If Dante had not done a deal more than borrow rhymes from Arnaut Daniel and theology from Aquinas he would not be published by Dent in the year of grace 1913. We might come to believe that the thing that matters in art is a sort of energy, something more or less like electricity or radioactivity, a force transfusing, wielding, and unifying. A force rather like water when it spurts up through very bright sand and sets it in swift motion." In this regard, José Lezama Lima: "The influences aren't causes that give place to effects, but effects that illuminate causes. . . . The scholars, who function as police on this subject, are more prone to casual chains than to illuminations. The impregnation, conjugation, and germination are more subtle forms of creation than casual developments. Besides, to continue A doesn't mean to follow A, since the history of human sensibility and culture is a magical continuation, not a following."

Would this knowledge be what moved the poets of al-Andalus—and many others, in other ways—to practice intertextuality? What did they seek to achieve? Perhaps to search for the reverberations, illuminations, and mysteries, that is, the other words that in the silence of the original text wait to add more mystery to mystery, creating new silences, that such mystery is infinite, sealed by the infinitude of the open word in the seal that expels it?

I will now read the approximate translation of a famous poem, "The Home of Love," that Yehuda Halevi probably composed at the beginning of the twelfth century. [The English version is by T. Carmi]:

Ever since You were the home of love
for me, my love has lived where You
have lived. Because of You, I have
delighted in the wrath of my enemies;
let them be, let them torment the one
whom You tormented. It was from You
that they learned their wrath, and I
love them, for they hound the wounded
one whom You struck down. Ever
since you despised me, I have despised
myself, for I will not honor what you
despise. So be it, until Your anger has
passed, and again You will redeem
Your own possession, which You once
redeemed.

In Hebrew, the poem follows a classic monorhythmic form, its vocabulary and images typical of love poetry. What is surprising is the last verse—"which You once redeemed" (your possession)—a concrete reference to the redemption of the Jewish people from slavery in Egypt. It is equally surprising that Yehuda Halevi's poem is an adaptation of an eighth-century love poem written in Arabic—except for the last verse.

Years ago, I dared to rewrite Yehuda Halevi's poem, no longer in relation to love or Jehovah, but to exile, mine:

you became my nest of love/and my love
lives where you live/the enemies
tormented me/let them be/let your ire be/

as long as I don't find my path to you/
my bones tremble embracing a stranger/
the foreigner of his own skin/
let it be/
as long as you don't absolve my pain/
seat me/redeem me/
rescue me from myself/

At times, I have a marvelous dream: that someone uses my own poem as spring-board, prolonging the writing initiated nine centuries ago, which echoes a poem of three centuries earlier. Poetry is infinite: it allows us to feel infinite, names and people endlessly transformed by radiance, sealed by the desire to feed and be fed.

Coming back to what brings us together, I believe that, unquestionably, there is a Jewish dimension in the work of all of us. I believe it is written with our body. Yet it is impossible, at least in my case, to define *lo judío*—what makes me Jewish in terms of subjectivity and the propensity to write. I don't know what pushed my Russian grandfather, a rabbi, facing the threat of a pogrom, to take out a scroll from a casket dating back to the mid-eighteenth century, a scroll containing the names of rabbis, his direct ancestors, and reading each of those names to his fourteen children, all silently sitting around the table. According to my mother, it was like reading Genesis: "Such and such begat such and such, who begat such and such, etc." This is proof that no pogrom can break the con-tinuity gathering them around the threatened table.

I remember the portrait of my grandfather, whom I never met, hanging on the wall in my parents' bedroom. Bearded, with eyes that saw far beyond what might be seen. The photograph left an imprint on me, I don't know how. My mother would say that her father was more handsome than I am, and that the one looking like him was my son. Mysteries of genealogy. Let us be confident in the mystery, without asking from it anything else: confident in its limits, always reaching back, always repeating, because it is the infinite that is given to us to pursue. There is so much life ahead of us, still.

Part Six

Dibaxu

(1994)

Scholium

I wrote the poems of *dibaxu* in Ladino, from 1983 to 1985. I'm of Jewish origin, but not Sephardic, which, I suppose, had to do with the endeavor. These poems are more than anything the culmination, or better the tributary, of *Quotes and Commentaries*, two books in a single volume I composed while in full exile, in 1978 and 1979, whose texts are in dialogue with sixteenth-century Spanish. The search for that language's substratum—which is our language, too—has been my obsession. The extreme solitude of exile pushed me to search for the deepest, most exiled roots of it. I can't explain it.

The access I got to poems by Clarisse Nicoïdski, a novelist in French and poet in Ladino, awakened in me an urge asleep in me, deaf, ready to wake up. What urge? Why was it asleep? Why deaf? Ladino syntax returned to me a lost candor: its diminutives, a tenderness toward others that is alive and full of comfort. Perhaps this volume is but a reflection on language from the burnt-out place of poetry.

I accompany the texts in present-day Spanish, not out of distrust for the reader's intelligence but for them to be read aloud in Spanish and listened to in Ladino, in the hope that maybe in between these two sounds a glimpse of the trembling past since El Cid comes back to us.

—J. G.

il batideru di mis bezus/
quero dizer: il batideru di mis bezus
si sinitirá in tu pasadu
cun mí in tu vinu/

avrindo la puerta dil tiempo/
tu sueniu
dexa cayer yuvia durmira/
dámila tu yuvia/

mi quedarí/quietu
in tu yuvia di sueniu/
londji nil pinser/
sin spantu/sin sulvidu

nila caza dil tiempo
sta il pasadu/
dibaxu di tu piede/
qui balia/

el temblor de mis labios/
quiero decir: el temblor de mis besos
se oirá en tu pasado
conmigo en tu vino/

abriendo la puerta del tiempo/
tu sueño
deja caer lluvia dormida/
dame tu lluvia/

me detendré/quieto
en tu lluvia de sueño/
lejos en el pensar/
sin temor/sin olvido/

en la casa del tiempo
está el pasado/
debajo de tu pie/
que baila/

I

the trembling of my lips/
I mean: the trembling of my kisses
will be heard in your past
with me in your wine/

opening the door of time/
your dream
allows sleeping rain to fall/
grant me your rain/

I will stop/still
in your rain of sleep/
far inside the thinking/
without fear/without oblivion/

in the house of time
is the past/
under your foot/
dancing

II

¿óndi sta la yave di tu curasón?/
il páxaru qui pasara es malu/
a mí no dixiera nada/
a mí dexara timblandu/

¿óndi sta tu corazón agora?/
un arvuli di spantu balia/
no más tengu ojus cun fanbre
y un djaru sin agua/

dibaxu dil cantu sta la boz/
dibaxu di la boz sta la folya
qu'il árvuli dexara
cayer di mi boca/

¿dónde está la llave de tu corazón?/
el pájaro que pasó es malo/
a mí no me dijo nada/
a mí me dejó temblando/

¿dónde está el corazón ahora?/
un árbol de espanto baila/
no tengo más que ojos con hambre
y un jarro sin agua/

debajo del canto está la voz/
debajo de la voz está la hoja
que el árbol dejó
caer de mi boca/

II

where is the key to your heart?/
the bird that flew away is evil/
it said nothing to me/
it left me trembling/

where is your heart now?/
a terrifying tree dances/
I have nothing but starving eyes/
and a pitch without water/

under the chant is the voice/
under the voice is the leaf
the tree allowed
to fall from my mouth/

III

l'amaniana arrelumbra a lus páxarus/
sta avierta/teni friscura/
la biviremus djuntu
cun il spantu dil pinser/

quirinsioza:
cayenta tu pasadu/
diz bezus y lus bezus dispartarán/
cayeremos cerca dil sol/

lembrara tu nagüita curilada/
tus floris curiladas/
yus bezus curiladus/
tu blancu curasón/

la mañana hace brillar a los pájaros/
está abierta/tiene frescura/
la beberemos junto
con el espanto del pensar/

querendona:
calienta lo pasado/
di besos y los besos despertarán/
caeremos cerca del sol/

recordé tus enaguas coloradas/
tus flores coloradas/
tus besos colorados/
tu blanco corazón/

III

the morning allows the birds to shine/
it is open/fresh/
together we shall drink from it
with the fright of thought/

beloved:
warm what is gone/
enunciate the kisses and the kisses shall awaken/
we shall descend near the sun/

I remembered your reddish petticoats/
your reddish flowers/
your reddish kisses/
your whitish heart/

IV

abáxati/si queris/veyi/
si queris/il páxaru
qui vola in mi boz
atan chitiu/

por il páxaru pasa un caminu
qui va a tus ojus/
aspira tu manu/
ay yerva ondi no stas/

durmi todu/
il páxaru/la boz/
il caminu/la yerva
qui amaniana viniera/

agáchate/si quieres/mira/
si quieres/el pájaro
que vuela en mi voz/
tan chico/

por el pájaro pasa un camino
que va a tus ojos/
espera tu mano/
hay hierba donde no estás/

todo duerme/
el pájaro/la voz/
el camino/la hierba
que mañana vino/

IV

bend down/if you want/look/
if you want/the bird
flying in my voice/
so small/

a path goes through the bird
targeting your eyes/
awaiting you hand/
grass springs where you aren't/

everything sleeps/
the bird/the voice/
the path/the grass/
brought by tomorrow/

V

quí lindus tus ojus/
il mirar di tus ojus más/
y más il airi di tu mirar londji/
nil airi stuvi buscando:

la lampa di tu sangri/
sangri di tu solombra/
tu solombra
sovri mi curasón/

qué lindos tus ojos/
y más la mirada de tus ojos/
y más el aire de tus ojos cuando lejos miras/
en el aire estuve buscando:

la lámpara de tu sangre/
sangre de tu sombra/
tu sombra
sobre mi corazón/

V

how beautiful your eyes/
and your sight even more/
and more the air of your eyes when you look asunder/
in the air I searched:

the lamp of your blood/
blood of your shadow/
your shadow
over my heart/

VI

folyas curiladas y verdis/
folyas secas/folyas friscas/
cayin di tu boz/
durmidas/

durmin dibaxu dil sol/
dibaxu di vos/
veyi cómu aspiran
qu'il spantu si amati/

il sol senti cayuer
tus folyas/qui
tiemblan nila nochi qui
insiende il bosco/

hojas coloradas y verdes/
hojas secas/hojas frescas/
caen de tu voz/
dormidas/

duermen debajo del sol/
debajo tuyo/
mira cómo esperan
que el espanto se apague/

el sol oye caer
tus hojas/que
tiemblan en la noche que
enciende el bosque/

VI

reddish and green leaves/
dry leaves/fresh leaves/
fall from your voice/
asleep/

asleep under the sun/
under you/
look at how they wait
for freight to be extinguished/

the sun hears
how your leaves fall/
trembling in the night that
illuminates the forest/

VII

la calor qui distruyi al pinser
si distruyi pinsendu/
la luz timbla
in tus bezus/y

queda al caminu/queda
al tiempo/londji/avri
lus bezus/dexa
yerva nil curasón quimadu/

si dispartara la yuvia
di un páxaru
qui aspira al mar
nil mar/

el calor que destruye al pensar
se destruye pensando/
la luz tiembla
en tus besos/y

detiene al camino/detiene
al tiempo/lejos/abre
los besos/deja
hierba en el corazón quemado/

se despertó la lluvia
de un pájaro
que espera al mar
en el mar/

VII

heat destroyed as it thinks
is destroyed thinking/
light trembles
in your kisses/and

stops the road/stops
time/far/opens
your kisses/leaves behind
grass in the burnt heart/

the rain woke up
from a bird
awaiting the sea
in the sea/

VIII

nil 'amaniana aviarta
in tus ojus abagan
lus animalis qui ti quimaran
adientru dil sueniu/

nunca dizin nada/
mi dexan sinizas/y
solu
cun il sol/

en la mañana abierta
lentamente por tus ojos pasan
los animales que te quemaron
adentro del sueño/

nunca dicen nada/
me dejan cenizas/y
solo
con el sol/

VIII

in the open morning
slowly the animals pass by
through your eyes that burned you
within the dream/

never utter a sound/
leaving me ashes/and
alone
with the sun/

IX

tu piede
pisa la nochi/suavi/
avri la yuvia/
avri il día/

la muerte no savi nada di vos/
tu piede teni yerva dibaxu
y una solombra ondi scrivi
il mar del vazío/

tu pie
pisa la noche/leve/
abre la lluvia/
abre el día/

la muerte nada sabe de vos/
tu pie tiene hierba debajo
y una sombra donde escribe
el mar del vacío/

IX

your foot
steps over the night/soft/
opening the rain/
opening the day/

death knows nothing of you/
your foot has grass under it
and a shadow where the sea
writes its void/

X

dizis avlas cun árvulis
tenin folyas qui cantan
y páxarus
qui djuntan sol/

tu silnziu
disparta
lus gritus
dil mundo/

dices palabras con árboles/
tienen hojas que cantan
y pájaros
que juntan sol/

tu silencio
despierta
los gritos
del mundo/

X

you utter words with trees/
they have singing leaves
and birds
gathering sun/

your silence
awakens
the world's
shrieks/

XI

partindu di tu ladu	partiendo de tu lado
discuvro	descubro
il nuevu mundu	el nuevo mundo
di tu ladu/	de tu lado/
tus islas comu lampas	tus islas como lámparas
cun una escuridad/	con una oscuridad/
yendu/viniendu/	yendo/viniendo/
nil tiempu/	en el tiempo/
in tu boz	en tu voz
il mar cayi	el mar cae
duluridu	dolorido
di mí/	de mí/

XI

departing from your side
I discover
the new world
of your side/

your islands like lamps
with darkness/
going/coming/
in time/

in your voice
the sea falls
suffering
from me/

XII

lu qui a mí dates	lo que me diste
es avla qui timbla	es palabra que tiembla
nila manu dil tiempo	en la mano del tiempo
aviarta para bever/	abierta para beber/
cayada	callada
sta la caza	está la casa
ondi nus bezamus	donde nos besamos
adientru dil sol/	adentro del sol/

XII

what you gave me
is trembling word
in the hand of time
open to drinking/

silenced
is the house
where we kissed
inside the sun/

XIII

eris
mi única avla/
no sé
tu nombi/

eres
mi única palabra/
no sé
tu nombre/

XIII

you are
my only word/
I know not
your name/

XIV

lu qui avlas	lo que hablas
dexa cayer	deja caer
un páxaru	un pájaro
qui li soy nidu/	y le soy nido/
il páxaru caya	el pájaro calla
adientru di mí/	en mí/
veyi	mira
lu qui faze di mí/	lo que hace de mí/

XIV

what you say
allows a bird
to fall
as I become its nest/

the bird is silent
inside me/
it finds out
what it makes of me/

XV

tu boz sta escura
di bezus qui a mí no dieras/
di bezus qui a mí no das/
la nochi es polvu dest'ixiliu/

tus bezus inculgan lunas
qui yelan mi caminu/y
timblu
dibaxu dil sol/

tu voz está oscura
de besos que no me diste/
de besos que no me das/
la noche es polvo de este exilio/

tus besos cuelgan lunas
que hielan mi camino/y
tiemblo
debajo del sol/

XV

your voice is dark
with kisses you never gave me/
with kisses you never give me/
night is dust of this exile/

your kisses dangle moons
freezing my path/and
I shake
under the sun/

XVI

cuando mi aya muridu
sintiré entudavía
il batideru
di tu saia nil vienti/

uno qui liyera istus versus
prieguntara: "¿cómu ansí?/
¿quí sintirás? ¿quí batideru?/
¿quí saia?/¿quí sienti?"/

li dixí qui cayara/
qui si sintara a la mesa cun mí/
qui biviera mi vinu/
qui scriviera istus versus:

"cuándo mi aya murido
sintiré estudavía
il batideru
di tu saia nil vienti"/

cuando esté muerto
oiré todavía
el temblor
de tu saya en el viento/

alguien que leyó estos versos
preguntó: "¿cómo así?/
¿qué oirás? ¿qué temblor?/
¿qué saya?/¿qué viento?"/

le dije que callara/
que se sentara a mi mesa/
que bebiera mi vino/
que escribiera estos versos:

"cuando esté muerto
oiré todavía
el temblor
de tu saya en el viento"/

XVI

when I am dead
I will still listen
to the shake
of your skirt in the wind/

someone who read these verses
asked: "how so?/
what will you hear?/what shake?/
what skirt?/what wind?"/

I told her to quiet down/
sit at my table/
drink my wine/
write these verses:

"when I am dead
I will still listen
to the shake
of your skirt in the wind"/

XVII

un vienti di separadus/
di bezus qui no mus diéramus/
acama il trigu di tu ventre/
sus asusenas cun sol/

vení/
o querré no aver nasidu/
trayi tu agua clara/
las ramas floreserán/

mira istu:
soy un niniu rompidu/
timblu nila nochi
qui cayi di mí/

un viento de separados/
de besos que no nos dimos/
doblega al trigo de tu vientre/
sus azucenas con sol/

ven/
o querré no haber nacido/
trae tu agua clara/
las ramas florecerán/

mira esto:
soy un niño roto/
tiemblo en la noche
que cae de mí/

XVII

a wind separating us/
with kisses never given/
subdues the wheat of your womb/
its white lilies with sun/

come/
or I will want not to have been born/
bring your clear water/
the branches will thrive/

look at this:
I am a broken child/
shaking in the night
falling from me/

XVIII

todu lu qui terra yaman	todo lo que llaman tierra
es tiempu/	es tiempo/
es aspira di vos/	es espera de vos/

XVIII

everything they call earth
is time/
awaiting you/

XIX

quirinsioza:
no ti vayas d'aquí/
di mi granu di arena/
desti minutu/

cuando stamus djuntus
il fuego cayi
sovri las ruinas
dil sol/

querendona:
no te vayas de aquí/
de mi grano de arena/
de este minuto/

cuando estamos juntos
el fuego cae
sobre las ruinas
del sol/

XIX

loving one:
don't depart from here/
from my grain of sand/
from this moment/

when we are together
fire falls
over the ruins
of the sun/

XX

no tenis puarta/yave/   no tienes puerta/llave/
no tenis sirradura/   no tienes cerradura/
volas di noche/   vuelas de noche/
volas di día/   vuelas de día/

lu amadu cría lu qui si amará/   lo amado crea lo que se amará/
comu vos/yave/   como tú/llave/
timblandu   temblando
nila puarta dil tiempo/   en la puerta del tiempo/

XX

you have no door/key/
you have no lock/
you fly by night/
you fly by day/

what is loved gives place to what will be loved/
like you/key/
shaking/
in the door of time/

XXI

sintí tu boz in mi vintana/
mi vintana no da a tu boz/
apenas si da al mundu/
¿cómu viniera tu boz?/

un páxaru nivadu
comi trigu
nil murmurio
dil sol/

oí tu voz en mi ventana/
mi ventana no da a tu voz/
apenas si da al mundo/
¿cómo vino tu voz?/

un pájaro nevado
come trigo
en el murmullo
del sol/

XXI

I heard your voice in my window/
my window doesn't surrender to your voice/
barely opening up to the world/
how did your voice arrive?/

a snowy bird
eats wheat
in the murmur
of the sun/

XXII

nila nochi
tu ventre queda astrus/
respira comu terra/
tu ventre es terra/

nil trigu di tu ventre
volan páxarus
qui cantan
in lu qui va a venir/

en la noche
tu vientre detiene astros/
respira como tierra/
tu vientre es tierra/

en el trigo de tu vientre
vuelan pájaros
que cantan
en lo que va a venir/

XXII

at night
your womb deters stars/
breathes like earth/
your womb is earth/

in the wheat of your womb
birds fly
singing
what is to come/

XXIII

in tu candor   en tu candor
sali il mundo dil mundo/ sale el mundo del mundo/
ista dicha es siega/   esta dicha es ciega/
mi pisa com'un buey/   me pisa como un buey/

XXIII

in your candor
the world emerges from the world/
this joy is blind/
stepping over me like an ox/

XXIV

amarti es istu:	amarte es esto:
un avla qui va a dizer/	una palabra que está por decir/
un arvulicu sin folyas	un arbolito sin hojas
qui da solombra/	que da sombra/

XXIV

loving you is this:
a word waiting to be said/
a small leafless tree
granting shade/

XXV

ista yuvia di vos
dexa cayer pidazus di tiempo/
pidazus d'infinitu/
pidazus di nus mesmos/

¿es por isu qui stamus
sin caza ni memoria?/
¿djuntus nil pinser?/
¿comu cuerpos al sol?/

tu lluvia
deja caer pedazos de tiempo/
pedazos de infinito/
pedazos de nosotros/

¿por eso estamos
sin casa ni memoria?/
¿juntos en el pensar?/
¿como cuerpos al sol?/

XXV

your rain
allows chunks of time to fall/
chunks of infinity/
chunks of us/

is that why we are
with no house or memory?/
together in thought?/
like bodies in the sun?/

XXVI

il diseu es un animal
todu vistidu di fuegu/
mi tení patas atan largas
qui yegan al sulvidu/

agora pinsu
qui un paxaricu in tu boz
arrastra
la caza dil otonio/

el deseo es un animal
todo vestido de fuego/
tiene patas tan largas
que llegan al olvido/

ahora pienso
que un pajarito en tu oz
arrastra
tu casa del otoño/

XXVI

desire is an animal
all dressed up with fire/
with such long legs
reaching oblivion/

I now think
of a small bird in your voice
carrying
the autumn house/

XXVII

mirandu il manzanu	mirando el manzano
vidi mi amor/	vi a mi amor/
crese/	crece/
no dize por quí/	no dice por qué/
no dize nada/	no dice nada/
il manzanu	el manzano
comu astrus	como astros
arde/	arde/

XXVII

looking at the apple tree
I saw my love
growing/
it doesn't say why/

it explains nothing/
the apple tree
like stars
burning/

XXVIII

¿cómu ti yamas?/
soy un siegu sintadu
nil atriu di mi diseu/
méndigu tiempo/

río di pena/
yoro d'alegría/
¿quí avla ti dezirá?/
¿quí nombri ti nombrará?/

¿cómo te llamas?/
soy un ciego sentado
en el atrio de mi deseo/
mendigo tiempo/

río de pena/
lloro de alegría/
¿qué palabra te dirá?/
¿qué nombre te nombrará?/

XXVIII

what is your name?/
I am a blind man sitting
in the atrium of my desire/
miserable time/

river of sorrow/
I cry out of joy/
what word will describe you?/
what name will name you?/

XXIX

no stan muridus lus páxarus
di nuestrus bezus/
stan moridus lus bezus/
lus páxarus volan nil verdi sulvidar/

pondrí mi spantu londji/
dibaxu dil pasadu/
qui arde
cayadu com'il sol/

no están muertos los pájaros
de nuestros besos/
están muertos los besos/
los pájaros vuelan en el verde olvidar/

pondré mi espanto lejos/
debajo del pasado/
que arde
callado como el sol/

XXIX

the birds of our kisses
are not dead/
the kisses are dead/
the birds coming back in the green forgetting/

my terror I will push far/
under the past/
burning
quit like the sun/

Part Seven

Worth It

(from Vale la pena [2001])

Medidas

El abuelo me mira desde
la foto de siempre, me mira
desde el fondo de Rusia y otras desgracias.
Desde el ghetto me mira. Dicen que
escribió una carta a Dios para
que inundara las casas de trigo,
de vino y de pan ázimo en Pascua,
y ató la carta a la pata de un pájaro
que voló de país en país buscando el cielo.
Me mira con las orejas lentas
de quien veló el espanto. Nunca
me levantó en sus brazos. Nunca
lo tuve, nunca
me tuvo, nunca
es la palabra entre los dos. Quiso
que la verdad paseara por la calle
y la cubrió con una máscara
para que la quisieran.
Esa máscara es su rostro en la foto.
Le habrá pedido a Dios que no
borre ni escriba nada porque
todo podría ser peor. La foto
está enferma, levanta
una humareda de brazos que no se encontrarán.
Empoza su linaje y
me sigue como un perro.

Measures

Grandfather looks at me from
the usual photo, he looks at me
from the depths of Russia and other misfortunes.
From the ghetto he looks at me. They
say he wrote a letter to God to
flood the houses with wheat,
wine and matzah on Passover,
and tied the letter to a bird's foot
which flew from country to country looking for heaven.
He looks at me with the slow sleepy ears
of someone who mourned terror. Grandfather
never picked me up in his arms. I never
had him, he never
had me. Never
is our agreed word. He wanted
truth to wander through the street
and covered it with a mask
so as to be wanted.
Grandfather must have asked God not
to commit anything into writing or erase it because
things could get worse. The photo
is sick, raising
a cloud of smoke made of arms unable to greet each other,
handcuffing its ancestry,
haunting me like a dog.

Nombres

Mi padre se llamaba José.
¿Por qué José?
¿Por qué se llamaba José? Tengo
que detenerlo en esta pregunta:
¿por qué te llamabas José? Ahí va
mi verte como si no quisieras
tener alma conmigo. La palabra
es una falta de palabra
en el rostro de una mujer.
La he visto en los desfiles del error.
Y ahora me siento a veces
a esperar su pérdida.
Cuando el día no es más
que esa enfermedad,
el sol no sola. El anuncio
incompleto de algo desconocido
baja con la tarde y veo
la cama donde muriste
y tu silencio que no se mueve.
¿Por qué José?
¿Por qué te llamabas José?

Names

My father's name was José.
Why José?
Why was he called José? I must
stop him with the question:
Why were you called José? There goes
my looking at you as if you never wanted
to share a soul with me. The word
is a loss of words
in a woman's face.
I have seen it in parades of error.
And sometimes I sit down
to wait for his absence.
When the day is nothing more
than such illness,
the sun refuses to sun. The unfinished
announcement of something unknown
descends with the afternoon as I see
the bed where you died
and your silence that won't die.
Why José?
Why were you called José?

Notes

In the 1990s, my teacher Raymond Scheindlin introduced me to medieval Hebrew poetry. The lessons have been with me ever since. I continued exploring the topic with my friend Ángel Sáenz-Badillos at Harvard and with Hillel Halkin during a couple of trips to Israel. And at Yale with the late María Rosa Menocal, and, subsequently, also at Yale, with my dear friend Peter Cole, whose life has been dedicated to translating poets like Samuel Hanagid, Yehuda Halevi, and other luminaries from Muslim and Christian Spain between 950 and 1492. He has delved into exploration of Kabbalah through the realm of poetry. This book is dedicated to him.

I wish to thank my editor extraordinaire Michael Millman, years ago at Penguin Classics and now at the University of New Mexico Press. His unyielding support has made this volume possible. To Anna Pohlod for shepherding the book through production and Norman Ware for his superb copyediting of the manuscript. Gracias to Carles Masdeu and Carina Pons of Agencia Literaria Carmen Balcells in Barcelona. And, of course, to Juan Gelman. We knew each other during the last years of his life, when I translated a few of his poems. Among other places, my renditions are included in *The FSG Book of Twentieth-Century Latin American Poetry* (Ilan Stavans, ed., 2011), the *New York Times* (June 20, 2014), and *I Am of the Tribe of Judah: Poems from Jewish Latin America* (Stephen A. Sadow, ed., 2024).

Part One. Quotes

These *Citas* and the poems in *Comentarios* appear in a single volume called *Citas y comentarios* (1982), which I used as my source. *Quotes* was written in Rome during November–December 1979. The book is dedicated "A mi país" (to my country), and in the front matter Gelman lists a number of people the individual poems are dedicated to, although he doesn't specify which to whom: Eduardo Galeano, Luise Rinser, Juan Carlos Calderón, Elba Izarduy, Paco Ibáñez, Jorge Cedrón, and Jorge Enrique Adoum.

Gelman wrote a total of forty-five Quotes, from which I have chosen seven.

In these poems, Gelman enters into a dialogue with Santa Teresa de Ávila (1515–1582), known as Santa Teresa de Jesús, the Carmelite nun canonized by Pope Gregory XV in 1622 and proclaimed the first female "Doctor of the Church" by Pope Paul VI on September 27, 1970. A conversa, she is best known for her autobiography, *La vida de la Santa Madre Teresa de Jesús* (The Life of the Holy Mother Teresa of Jesus, composed in Ávila, Spain, between 1562 and 1565 but published posthumously); *Camino de perfección* (The Way of Perfection, 1567), written at the direction of her confessor; and, crucially for Gelman, the spiritual manual *Las moradas; o, El castillo interior* (1577). Santa Teresa's poems are a study in contrast. This is an emblematic—and famous—Gelmanesque stanza, followed by my translation:

> Vivo sin vivir en mí,
> y tan alta vida espero,
> que muero porque no muero.

> I live unliving in me
> and such exalted life I wish,
> I die for undying.

There are two previous translations of *Quotes*, one of them partial: Hardie St. Martin rendered I, IV, VI, XV, and XXXV (*Dark Times Filled with Light*, 109–13). And the entire collection was translated by Lisa Rose Bradford in *Between Words: Juan Gelman's "Public Letter"* (2010).

Gelman's deep reading of Santa Teresa de Ávila's *Las moradas; o, El castillo interior* results in a dialogue about exile, contemplation, and wholeness. Although it is challenging to determine their precise provenance, "Quote II," "Quote VIII," "Quote XIX," "Quote XXVI," "Quote XXX," "Quote XXXI," and "Quote XLV" are rewritings of the sections "Moradas Primeras," "Moradas Segundas," and "Moradas Quintas."

Part Two. Commentaries

My source is *Citas y comentarios* (1982). Gelman wrote a total of sixty-five *comentarios*, from which I have chosen five, which he wrote in 1978 while in Rome, Madrid, Paris, Zurich, Geneva, and Calella de la Costa, Spain. Some are in dialogue with Santa Teresa de Ávila, others with San Juan de la Cruz, and a few more with an assortment of figures, ancient and contemporary, such as biblical kings and prophets, and poets like Charles Baudelaire and painters like Vincent van Gogh. The word *comentarios* can also be rendered as "midrashim" because of their importance in Jewish tradition. A midrash is a mode of interpretation prominent in the Talmudic literature. The mode has mutated over time to become a flexible, multigenre hermeneutical tool for Jews to engage with a variety of canonical texts.

San Juan de la Cruz (1542–1591), of converso blood, was a Carmelite mystic active during the Counter-Reformation in Spain; he was mentored by and corresponded with Santa Teresa de Ávila and was canonized by Pope Benedict XIII in 1726. San Juan de la Cruz is best known for *Cántico espiritual* (Spiritual Canticle), an eclogue designed as a search by a bride, the human soul, for her bridegroom, Jesus Christ. There is a direct link to the biblical Song of Songs. San Juan de la Cruz wrote the first thirty-one stanzas of his eclogue while imprisoned in the Carmelite monastery of Toledo because his relationship with Santa Teresa was considered inappropriate, then he added more stanzas. Some scholars suggest that the second section was written by another author. San Juan de la Cruz's other major work is *Noche oscura del alma* (Dark Night of the Soul), estimated to have been written in 1578 or 1579. A few years later, the author wrote commentaries to the first two stanzas of *Noche oscura* and the first line of the third. Again, the theme is the journey of the human soul in search of the divine.

There are three previous English translations of Gelman's *Comentarios*, two of them partial: Joan Lindgren renders I, VI, and XX (*Unthinkable Tenderness*, 47–52), Lisa Rose Bradford offers a full translation in *Commentaries and Citations* (2010), and Hardie St. Martin renders I, II, III, IV, VII, XI, XVII, XIX, XXVII, XXVIII, and LXIII (*Dark Times Filled with Light*, 94–108). As in the case of *Quotes*, the *Commentaries* are difficult to trace. Some are linked to Santa Teresa de Ávila. Three that I translate in this volume are connected with San Juan de la Cruz: "Commentary XXVIII," "Commentary XLII," and "Commentary XLIII." All deal with the arduous path leading to emotional exaltation.

The last two commentaries that I translate have different inspirations: "Commentary LVIII" is a rewriting of a noncultic psalm that in the Bible is attributed to King David (from *The Penguin Book of Hebrew Verse*, 168–71), particularly three lines "as the wild asses quench their thirst/," "you fix the branches singing songs of the earth/," and "wrapped in splendor you remove all darkness."

Gelman isn't interested in King David's prowess as a political leader but in the psalms attributed to him. Psalms are songs of gratitude to the divine, but in Gelman they metamorphose into explorations of exile. His source is Psalm 104, a lengthy hymn of self-exhortation and a meditation on God's providential justice, which he distills to just eight lines. In *Com/positions*, Gelman includes three more psalmic variations.

"Commentary XLVIII" is inspired by the forewarnings of the Jerusalemite prophet Isaiah, son of Amoz. A number of hands, each belonging to a different period, took part in the composition of the book of Isaiah. Hence, it is difficult to know Isaiah as a biblical character. Gelman uses various sections as inspiration, including Chapter 24.

Part Three. Com/positions

These variations are part of *Com/posiciones* (1986). My source is Gelman's *Otromundo: Antología 1956–2007*. The volume is dedicated to José Ángel Valente (1929–2000), a Spanish poet and scholar and Gelman's friend. Among other volumes, Valente's poetry is compiled in *Poemas de Lázaro* (Poems of Lazarus, 1960), *Interior con figuras* (Interior with Silhouettes, 1976), and *Tres lecciones de tinieblas* (Three Lessons on Darkness, 1980). He was awarded both the Premio Príncipe de Asturias and the Premio Reina Sofía. Gelman shared with him a passion for the work of Santa Teresa de Ávila and San Juan de la Cruz.

In *Com/positions*, Gelman engaged with an assortment of biblical and medieval poetry. What attracted him to it wasn't the religious dimension but the exilic condition of the original authors, the way they wrestled with longing and resilience. Lindgren translates the exergue, "The Cradle," "Psalm," "What Will Come to Pass," "The Expulsed," "The Prisoner," "Song," "The Battle," and "In Prison" (*Unthinkable Tenderness*, 146–60). Hardie St. Martin translates the exergue as well as "The Door," "Faithless," "The Banished," "The Sleeper," "The Prisoner," "The Judgment," "The Moment," "Moments during the Battle of Alfuente," "The Jasmine," "Invitation," "On Learning That My Enemy Has Died," "The Phoenix," and "When" (*Dark Times Filled with Light*, 152–70). And Lisa Rose Bradford translates the entire collection in *Com/positions* (2013). I have occasionally drawn from these renditions.

Although no reference is listed in Gelman's book, his principal source in reimagining medieval Hebrew poetry is the Hebrew-English anthology *The Penguin Book of Hebrew Verse* (1981), edited by T. Carmi. Albeit less frequently, he also used José María Millás Vallicrosa's *La poesía sagrada hebraicoespañola* (1940). My own sources include, in Spanish, Ángel Sáenz-Badillos's *Literatura hebrea en la España medieval* (1991), and in English, Raymond Scheindlin's *The Gazelle: Medieval Hebrew Poems on God, Israel, and the Soul* (1991); María Rosa Menocal's *The Ornament of the World: How Muslims, Jews, and Christians Created a Culture of Tolerance in Medieval Spain* (2002); Peter Cole's *The Dream of the Poem: Hebrew Poetry from Muslim and Christian Spain, 950–1492* (2007); and *The Poetry of Kabbalah: Mystical Verse from the Jewish Tradition*, also edited by Cole (2012).

Gelman returns to the noncultic Davidic psalms. His "Psalm I" loosely connects with Psalm 122 and "Psalm III" with Psalm 130. The poem "The Bull" is a meditation on the biblical prophet Amos, considered one of the twelve "minor" prophets. A sheep herder and sycamore farmer, he states in Amos 7:14 (in Robert Alter's translation): "No prophet am I, nor the son of a prophet am I." Amos's grief and solitude is the hook Gelman found compelling. His poem "The Ox" starts: "grief enwraps me/am I tied to you?/for me to plow my solitude?/"

The source of "The Calling" is the book of Ezekiel, whose hallucinatory visions of angels and other celestial creatures fascinated Gelman. The imagery comes from Ezekiel 21, including the lines "do you scream and howl like one with disjointed loins?/" and "so that the heart faints and tumbling blocks abound?/" from Robert Alter's translation (*The Hebrew Bible: Prophets*, 1112).

Arguably the biblical character closest to Gelman's emotional arch is Job, as he was for John Milton, Franz Kafka, Fyodor Dostoevsky, and others. The book of Job, part of *Ketuvim* (The Writings), is both unique and mysterious. Unique because it doesn't feature the Israelites as protagonists, but features one Israelite as an average person from the land of Uz. And mysterious because it is composed as a powerful poetic debate between Job and God, and between Job and a handful of his friends. Historically, we know nothing about the book's author and protagonist, except through the actual narrative, which enwraps the reader. The death of Gelman's son and daughter-in-law, his exile during the Cold War, his trials and tribulations in Spain, France, Mexico, and elsewhere, all feel Job-like. "The Phoenix" springs from Job 29–18: "In my nest I shall breathe my last, and my days will abound like the sand." I use Robert Alter's English-language rendition in *The Hebrew Bible: The Writings*, 539.

The Dead Sea Scrolls are a series of papyri discovered in 1946 and 1956 at the Qumran Caves, in Ein Feshkha, in the West Bank. They are an expression of the rich ecosystem of religious life in the period known as Second Temple Judaism, roughly at the time when Jesus Christ preached his gospel. Some of the parchments are in Hebrew, others in Aramaic and Greek. They pertain to the sect of the Essenes, although some interpreters suggest that they belong to other sects. A few writings are apocalyptic in nature, describing the end of times and the preparations required in order to face Armageddon. Gelman dedicates a couple of poems to them: "Trees" (Dead Sea Scrolls) and "What Will Come" (Dead Sea Scrolls) are inspired by two English translations by T. Carmi in *The Penguin Book of Hebrew Verse*: "The Parable of the Trees" (187–88) and "The Mystery to Come" (186).

The Hekhalot hymns (the Hebrew word *hekhalot* means palace) were anonymous compositions by Jewish mystics dating to the fourth century. They are part of what is known as Merkavah mysticism, which coalesced around the image of the chariot (*merkavah*) in the book of Ezekiel, with which the Prophet Ezekiel describes his elaborate vision of the divine. Hekhalot mysticism is equally linked to the journey of Moses to receive the Torah. Samples of early Hekhalot hymns are in the apocryphal fourth book of Ezra, written around 100 CE. This is the King James Version:

> O Lord, thou that dwellest in everlastingness [Hekhalot] which beholdest from above things in the heaven and in the air; whose throne [Merkavah] is inestimable; whose glory may not be comprehended; before whom the hosts of angels stand with trembling, whose service is conversant in wind and fire. (4 Ezra 8:21–22a)

Gelman rewrites a couple of these Hekhalot hymns. The originals, along with their English translations, are found in *The Penguin Book of Hebrew Verse*. The poem "Morning Prayer" is based on "Hymn for the Descent to the Merkava" (195), and "Let Us Hope" follows closely "The Throne of Glory Addresses the King" (198–99).

The first significant medieval Hebrew poet, and among the most influential, is Samuel Hanagid (993–1056). A renown Talmudist, military figure, and states-man born in Córdoba, Hanagid fled the Andalusian capital when the Berbers destroyed it in 1013. In Hebrew, the term *hanagid* means "the Prince," a title he received because of his role as vizier in 1038, the year when he began his com-mand of the armies of Granada against Seville and its allies. A few of his poems, written to his son Yosef in the battlefield, are full of war scenery and address the savagery and viciousness of revenge in that environment. Hanagid died during one of his military campaigns. Three of Gelman's poems are inspired by, and closely follow, Carmi's renditions in *The Penguin Book of Hebrew Verse*: "The

Moment" is based on "The Moment" (285), including the line "Rejoice, for God has brought/you to your fiftieth year in the world!"; "Scenes from the Battle of Alfuente" follows closely "The Battle of Alfuente" (286–87); and "On Learning of My Enemy's Death" is based on "On Learning of His Enemy's Death" (289–91). Aside from Carmi's anthology, my source is Peter Cole's *Selected Poems of Shmuel HaNagid* (1996).

Known in Latin as Avicebron, Solomon ibn Gabirol (ca. 1022–ca. 1070) was a neo-Platonic philosopher and poet, the author of *Keter Malkhut* (The Kingly Crown) as well as *Mekor Hayim* (Crown of Life), which in Latin is titled *Fons vitae* (the book was written in Arabic). According to Moses ibn Ezra, ibn Gabirol had an irascible temperament, which dominated his intellect. He likely suffered from lupus vulgaris, a skin disease that results in disfigurement. In autobiographical sections, he describes himself as a midget. I have chosen three poems of Gelman's selection: "The Door" is based on "To God" (*The Penguin Book of Hebrew Verse*, 313–14); "The Loss" relates to "The Faithless Woman" (312–13), as in the line "she whose neck is so lovely with its ornaments"; and "The Witnesses" uses a number of lines from "The Testimony of Beauty" (313), such as "How can yellow noon unfold the rosy dawn?" and "Beauty is vain, and charm a delusion." Another useful source is Raymond Scheindlin's *Vulture in a Cage: Poems by Solomon ibn Gabirol* (2016).

Gelman felt an affinity toward Yehuda Halevi (1075–1141), arguably the most famous Hebrew poet of the Jewish "Golden Age" in poetry. A proto-Zionist, he left a comfortable life in Spain when he moved to Palestine. Long considered lost, several of Halevi's writings were discovered by Moldavian-born British-American rabbi, scholar, and educator Solomon Schechter at the end of the nineteenth century, in the Cairo Genizah. This is considered one of the most important modern-era archaeological findings related to Hebrew writings. Halevi's most famous work is his *Songs of Zion*. A multifaceted figure, Halevi wrote in Arabic and Hebrew, leaving behind an extensive poetic oeuvre as well as a canonical work in philosophy called *Sefer ha-Kuzari* (The Book of Argument and Proof in Defense of the Despised Faith), which was completed in 1139–1140. The Khazars were a semi-nomadic Turkic people. In the late sixth century, they established a major commercial empire covering the southeastern section of what is today Russia, southern Ukraine, Crimea, and Kazakhstan. According to legend, the Khazar king converted the Khazars to Judaism after pondering which of the three major Abrahamic religions, Judaism, Christianity, or Islam, was the best. Halevi's *Kuzari* is shaped as a dialogue between a Jewish scholar (the *haver*) and the king of the Khazars, at the end of which the king makes his decision. I have chosen six poems in which Gelman is in dialogue with Halevi: "Prayer," based on "The Home of Love" (*The Penguin Book of Hebrew Verse*, 333–34), as stated in *"Lo judío* in Spanish-Language Literature"; "To Wash," connecting with "The Laundress" (343); and "Song," relating to "Song of Farewell" (343–44). "The Country of the Dove," "To Say," and "The Blind Man" come from other sources. Useful sources are, in Spanish, Máximo José Kahn and Juan Gil-Albert's *Yehudá Haleví* (1987), and, in English, Raymond Scheindlin's *The Song of the Distant Dove: Judah Halevi's Pilgrimage* (2007) and Hillel Halkin's biography *Yehuda Halevi* (2010).

Yehuda al-Harizi, originally from Toledo, Spain, was a poet, translator, and traveler; he was educated in Castile and died in Aleppo, Syria, in 1225. He rendered into Hebrew (from Arabic) Maimonides's *Guide for the Perplexed*, which he titled *Moreh Nevukhim*.

An example of Gelman's Pessoan mode, the poet Eliezer ben Jonon (1130–1187) is an invention, a heteronym. The biographical dates insert him in the context of early medieval Hebrew poetry, between Samuel Hanagid and Solomon ibn Gabirol. But the locations Gelman concocts—Mainz, Toledo, and Provence—place him in a multitude of sites of exile between Germany, Spain, and France. Cynthia Gabbay, in her essay *"Com/posiciones*: Los poemas de Eliezer ben Jonon: Heteronimia, simbolismo y exilio" (in *La memoria de la dictadura*, edited by Fernando Moreno, 2006, 337–45), explores aspects of this Pessoan experiment.

Joseph ben Samuel Tsarfati (d. 1547), known as Giuseppe Gallo, was a poet and scholar during the Italian Renaissance. He was the first to translate *La Celestina* (1499) by the converso writer and lawyer Fernando de Rojas, into Hebrew, in 1507. A physician, he led an eventful life, which included being accused of being a papal spy in Constantinople, which resulted in his imprisonment. Tsarfati's introductory poem to his translation is all that remains of it. A total of 230 poems by Tsarfati survive. In Hebrew, Tsarfati's last name (at times spelled Zarfati) means "from Spain." His poem "The Judgment" is based on T. Carmi's English version of "The Judgement of Time," from *The Penguin Book of Hebrew Verse* (455).

Isaac Luria (1534–1572), known in Hebrew by his anagram Ha'ari (the lion), was a major Kabbalist. He was born in Jerusalem and brought to Egypt, eventually settling in Safed. After his death, a circle of initiated followers developed a system of thought based on his teachings. Initially, Luria was known as an ecstatic poet. "The Orphan" resembles "To His Self" from *The Penguin Book of Hebrew Verse* (471), except that Luria's poem addresses issues of disassociation, whereas Gelman transforms the poem into a meditation on gratitude to creation. At the end of the poem, Gelman stresses Luria's exilic journey by listing the places he lived in: Jerusalem, Alexandria, and Safed. "Where" and "There" are also grounded in "To His Self." In the former, Gelman includes the lines "in what distress do you shield me?/" and "I will cry out my verses about you in solitude/." In the latter, he uses the word "cabeza" for "Keter," one of the Sephirot in Kabbalah, which are ten sources of emanation through which the Ein Sof (in Hebrew, "Without End," meaning the Infinite) reveals itself. Following the structure of Plotinus, the Sephirot as vessels connect the physical and spiritual realms. I have therefore translated "cabeza" as crown.

Part Four. Letter to My Mother

This unusually lengthy poem by Gelman appeared as *Carta a mi madre* (1989). It is dedicated to Gelman's sister, Teodora. My source is *Otromundo: Antología 1956–2007*. Gelman's mother's name was Paulina Burichson. The poem was written in Geneva and Paris between June 1984 and November 1987. There are two complete English translations of the poem, one by Joan Lindgren (*Unthinkable Tenderness*, 169–80), the other by Hardie St. Martin (*Dark Times Filled with Light*, 173–79). Lindgren presents her translation as prose, meaning she doesn't follow Gelman's line breaks.

Gelman's *Carta abierta* (Open Letter, 1980), written in 1980 when he lived in Paris and Rome, serves as a coda to his journey of Jewish exploration. The volume is dedicated to his son, Marcelo Ariel Gelman Schuberoff. The running theme is Marcelo's killing by the Argentine military junta. In the Buenos Aires newspaper *Página/12*, Gelman published "Carta abierta a mi nieta o nieto" (Open Letter to My Granddaughter or Grandson, April 12, 1995), in which he said that his grandchild was born in 1976 and that they had never met. He assumed that the child had been born in a concentration camp, probably the one known as Pozo de Quilmes. The letter generated a number of responses, which ultimately led to an encounter between Gelman and his granddaughter, who changed her name to María Macarena Gelman García to acknowledge her biological parents. Born in Montevideo on November 1, 1976, she is now a Uruguayan activist and politician. In "Carta abierta a mi nieta o nieto," Gelman states:

> It is very strange for me to talk to you of my children as the parents you never had. I don't know if you are male or female. I know you

were born. Father Fiorello Cavalli, of the Secretariat of the Vatican State, assured me of that fact, in February 1978. Since then, I have asked myself what your fate might have been. I am overwhelmed by a couple of conflicting ideas. On the one hand, I wonder if you call "father" a corrupt military or police man, or a friend of your parents' killers. On the other, I always wished, whatever your home ended up being, for you to have been raised and educated well and given much love. Still, I never stopped thinking some kind of fault or hole would exist in the love they granted you, not because those who brought you up aren't your biological parents—as it is said today—but because they somehow would have been aware of your story and how they falsified it. I suppose they have lied to you a lot.

All these years, I also have thought what to do if I found you, if I would tear you away from the home you had or talked to your adopted parents to make an agreement allowing me to see you and accompany you, always on the premise that you would know who you are and where you come from. The dilemma came up whenever the possibility arose of the Grandmothers of the Plaza de Mayo having found you. I was worried you would be too young—or not young enough—to understand what had happened, understand that the parents you thought were your parents or maybe you loved weren't your parents. I was worried your developing subjectivity would suffer a double wound. But now you're a grownup. You can understand who you are and can decide what to do with what you are. The grandmothers have developed a blood bank allowing people to determine, with scientific precision, the origin of the children of the disappeared. Your origin.

In a note attached to the poem in the original edition of *Si dulcemente* (If Gently), Gelman writes: "On August 24, 1976, my son Marcelo Ariel and his wife Claudia, pregnant, were kidnapped in Buenos Aires by a military unit. As in dozens of other cases, the military dictatorship never officially recognized these desaparecidos. It talked of 'ausentes para siempre' [forever absent]. Until I see their corpses or assassin, I will never consider them dead."

There are three English translations of *Open Letter*, two of them partial. Sections XIII and XVII were rendered by Joan Lindgren (*Unthinkable Tenderness*, 31–35). The entire collection was translated by Lisa Rose Bradford in *Between Words: Juan Gelman's "Public Letter"* (2010), and sections IV, XVI, and XX were translated by Hardie St. Martin (*Dark Times Filled with Light*, 79–84).

Part Five. *Lo judío* and Spanish-Language Literature

Written in New York on June 5, 1992, this keynote address was delivered by Gelman in Buenos Aires as part of the Cuarto Encuentro de Escritores Judíos Latinoamericanos, which took place from August 9 to 12, 1992. The edited transcription was subsequently printed in the journal *Hispamérica* 21, no. 62 (August 1992): 83–90, edited by Argentine literary scholar Saúl Sosnowski.

The essay "The Last Letter" was published in *Página/12*, February 11, 1999.

In the lecture, Gelman reflects on a variety of topics central to his exploration of Ladino themes, from the technique used by the Hebrew poets of al-Andalus of inserting biblical quotations and verses in poems or building entire poems around those motifs, to the French school of literary criticism promoted by Jacques Derrida and Julia Kristeva predicated on intertextuality as a game of literary connections. Gelman mentions Russian philosopher and literary critic Mikhail Bakhtin (1895–1975), author of, among other books, *Problems of Dostoevsky's Poetics* (1929). He also refers to French novelist and theorist Jean Ricardou (1932–2016), whose book *Problèmes du nouveau roman* (1967) studies the works of Michel Butor, Claude Ollier, Alain Robbe-Grillet, Claude Simon, and Philippe Sollers. There are also references to American poet Ezra Pound (1885–1975), especially to his essay "The Serious Artist," although not to his anti-Semitism, and to Cuban novelist José Lezama Lima (1910–1976), author of *Paradiso* (1966).

Gelman quotes Spanish linguist, anthropologist, and historian Julio Caro Baroja (1914–1995), who taught at Oxford University and the University of the Basque Country in northern Spain. He wrote an influential three-volume study on the Jews of Spain called *Los judíos en la España moderna y contemporánea* (1962). The quotation in the lecture comes from Caro Baroja's *La sociedad criptojudía en la corte de Felipe IV* (1963).

The discussion about the technique to insert biblical references in medieval Hebrew texts opposes, on the one hand, Dunash ha-Levi ben Labrat (ca. 920–ca. 990), a midrashic commentator and grammarian who wrote *Teshuvot Dunash* and the liturgical poems *D'ror Yiqra* and *D'vai Haser*, and on the other, Menahem ibn Saruk (ca. 920–ca. 970), also a philologist and the author of one of the first dictionaries of the Hebrew language. Their disagreement was on grammatical rules and religious standards. Gelman discusses the antagonism between Labrat and Saruk in his essay "Cruces," published in *Página/12*, January 6, 2002, and collected in *Miradas* (2004).

The translation of Yehuda Halevi's poem "The Home of Love" by T. Carmi in *The Penguin Book of Hebrew Verse* (333–34) is the one Gelman uses as his source.

Gelman mentions Gershom Scholem (1897–1982), a German-born Israeli scholar of Kabbalah, who taught for years at Hebrew University in Jerusalem. A friend of literary critic Walter Benjamin, Scholem is the author, among other books, of *Major Trends in Jewish Mysticism* (1941), a foundation for Gelman's understanding of Kabbalah.

In its structure, *"Lo judío* in Spanish-Language Literature" reminds me of Borges's lecture "The Argentine Writer and Tradition," delivered (also in Buenos Aires) in 1951 and, like Gelman's lecture, subsequently transcribed and edited. It explores the freedom Argentine writers should embrace by rejecting localism and seeking to explore universal topics in their work. It is one of a series of pieces in which Borges discusses diasporic Jewish culture. In this regard, a crucial paragraph argues (in James E. Irby's translation):

> What is our Argentine tradition? I believe we can answer this question easily and that there is no problem here. I believe our tradition is all of Western culture, and I also believe we have a right to this tradition, greater than that which the inhabitants of one or another Western nation might have. I recall here an essay of Thorstein Veblen, the North American sociologist, on the pre-eminence of Jews in Western culture. He asks if this pre-eminence allows us to conjecture about the innate superiority of the Jews, and answers in the negative; he says that they are outstanding in Western culture because they act within that culture and, at the same time, do not feel tied to it by any special devotion; "for that reason," he says, "a Jew will always find it easier than a non-Jew to make innovations in Western culture"; and we can say the same of the Irish in English culture. In the case of the Irish, we have no reason to suppose that the profusion of Irish names in British literature and philosophy is due to any racial pre-eminence, for many of those illustrious Irishmen (Shaw, Berkeley, Swift) were the descendants of Englishmen, were people who had no Celtic blood; however, it was sufficient for them to feel

Irish, to feel different, in order to be innovators in English culture. I believe that we Argentines, we South Americans in general, are in an analogous situation; we can handle all European themes, handle them without superstition, with an irreverence which can have, and already does have, fortunate consequences.

While Gelman's argument is different (medieval Hebrew poets shape their oeuvre by astutely quoting from biblical texts), the thesis is also about universality: writers embrace atemporal themes by establishing connections with their precursors and successors.

Part Six. *Dibaxu*

In the early 1990s, Gelman decided to teach himself Ladino. The result was *Dibaxu* (1994). I have included all twenty-nine poems. Gelman writes in the scholium that he wrote the poems during 1983–1985. At its core, the volume is an exercise in self-translation. Gelman produced two originals, one to be read aloud, the other to be listened to. I have written on the topic in *Self-Translation: Meditations on Language* (2018).

Clarisse Nicoïdski (1938–1996) was a Franco-Jewish poet, opera librettist, and novelist. Gelman discovered his passion for Ladino after reading her poems, which are collected in a bilingual Ladino/Spanish edition, *El color del tiempo* (2014). "Angst" springs from Nicoïdski's "ansia," written in Ladino:

cumiendo mi luz
biviendu mi soplo
mi arasgas
ni la curilada oscuridá
di mi pinser
di mi temblor
qui dizirás?
in tu boca
as palavras puedin ser piedras
i puedin ser palavras
qui dizirás?

My translation:

> eating my light
> drinking my blow
> you tear me apart
> not even the twisted darkness
> of my thought
> of my trembling
> what would you say?
> not your mouth
> words might be stones
> and might be words
> what would you say?

And another translation as if through Gelman's eyes:

> sucking the light/
> freezing my breath/
> angst/
> you rip me apart/
> a frenzy of thoughts/
> is anything left of me?/
> in my mouth
> words become stones/
> and back to words/
>
>
> what shall you say?/
> or I/
> to you/stranger in me/
> making me stranger/
> or you?/
>
>
> after I surrender/
> then what?/

In the scholium to *Dibaxu*, Gelman states: "The access I got to poems by Clarisse Nicoïdski, a novelist in French and poet in Ladino, awakened in me an urge asleep in me, deaf, ready to wake up. What urge? Why was it asleep? Why deaf? Ladino syntax returned to me a lost candor: its diminutives, a tenderness toward others that is alive and full of comfort. Perhaps this volume is but a reflection on language from the burnt-out place of poetry."

Part Seven. Worth It

From the volume *Vale la pena* (2001). The only two poems in this section, both exploring Gelman's genealogical tree, are "Measures" and "Names." In an interview with the journal *Sudestada* (2002), Gelman suggested that the title was inspired by a verse by Francisco Urondo (1930–1976), who, like Gelman, was part of the Montoneros and whose poetry, in Gelman's words, "is motorized by antithesis and paradox, mechanisms capable of apprehending the contradictory nature of reality."

Index of First Lines

Entries in italic text indicate Spanish first lines. Entries in bold text indicate Ladino first lines.